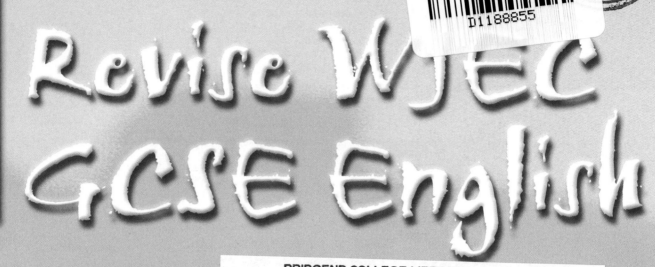

Revise WJEC GCSE English

IMAGINE

persuade

PROSE

Roger Lane

WJEC CBAC

OXFORD
UNIVERSITY PRESS

OXFORD
UNIVERSITY PRESS

Great Clarendon Street, Oxford OX2 6DP

Oxford University Press is a department of the University of Oxford.
It furthers the University's objective of excellence in research, scholarship,
and education by publishing worldwide in

Oxford   New York

Auckland   Cape Town   Dar es Salaam   Hong Kong   Karachi
Kuala Lumpur   Madrid   Melbourne   Mexico City   Nairobi
New Delhi   Shanghai   Taipei   Toronto

With offices in

Argentina   Austria   Brazil   Chile   Czech Republic   France   Greece
Guatemala   Hungary   Italy   Japan   Poland   Portugal   Singapore
South Korea   Switzerland   Thailand   Turkey   Ukraine   Vietnam

Oxford is a registered trade mark of Oxford University Press
in the UK and in certain other countries

© Roger Lane

British Library Cataloguing in Publication Data

Data available

ISBN-13: 978-0-19-831886-6
ISBN-10: 0-19-831886-3

3 5 7 9 10 8 6 4

and typeset by Mike Brain Graphic Design Limited
Printed at Alden Press Ltd, Oxford

Acknowledgements

The author would like to thank:
Hugh Lester – for generous help
and support, and
Elizabeth Evans – for yet more
sample answers.

The Publisher would like to thank the following
for permission to reproduce photographs:
Corel Professional Photos: p25; Photodisc: p32.

Maps are by Oxford Design and Illustrators.

We are grateful for permission to include the
following copyright material in this book:
Kazuo Ishiguro: Extracts from *The Remains of the Day*
(Faber & Faber, 1989), reprinted by permission of the publishers.
Martin Plimmer: Extract from *King of the Castle* (Ebury, 2002),
reprinted by permission of The Random House Group Limited.
Simon Potter: Extracts and picture from 'An Open Road To Death'
first published in *The Times* 08.06.03, reprinted by permission
of N I Syndication Limited.

Although we have tried to trace and contact copyright holders before
publication, in some cases this has not been possible. If notified we will be
pleased to rectify any errors or omissions at the earliest opportunity.

This book is dedicated to the memory of Wyn Roberts

Contents

To the student

This guide helps to prepare you for the GCSE examination papers at the end of your WJEC English course. It will take you step-by-step through the reading and writing sections of English Paper 1 and Paper 2. It caters for both Foundation and Higher tier candidates by providing a set of papers for each tier, focusing on significant differences between the demands of the tiers, but also showing how the tiers test the same skills in similar ways. If you are a Foundation tier candidate, you could, perhaps should (!), also attempt the Higher tier sections of this guide; and vice-versa.

The guide works alongside the Oxford/WJEC *Students' Book*, *Teacher's Guide* and *Coursework Guide*, but it should help you perfectly well if you use it as a 'stand-alone' revision aid without any reference to the other titles. It should help whether you are reading it just days before your exams or with a few months to prepare. You should find that it works without the intervention of your teacher, tutor or parents, although none of them is banned from reading it!

The next page maps out the GCSE English course to show where the final English exams fit into it. For many of you, GCSE English Literature will also feature both as another qualification and as an overlap with English (especially in coursework). There is a separate *GCSE English Literature Revision Guide*. Written coursework and Speaking & Listening are covered in the *Coursework Guide*.

The sample answers in this guide are all quite impressive, not to frighten you, nor to make you feel inadequate, but to make you aware of what is possible in response to the questions and tasks set. (The *Teacher's Guide* contains many sample answers showing work at a range of different grades.) Candidates do display remarkable quality under examination conditions and also manage to sustain it at some length. Generally, the sample answers go beyond what is required for full marks!

The best way to use this guide would be to read the specimen questions and then to answer them under pressure of time before studying the sample responses. However, reading the guide and simply taking in the advice might be the most useful approach if your exams are approaching very soon. Whichever approach you adopt, all the very best of luck in the 'real thing' – remember to keep calm, use the time fully and concentrate on giving your best possible performance. You might be better than you imagine. Good luck!

Roger Lane

ROGER LANE

How the English exams fit into the GCSE English course

English coursework (20% of the assessment)

♣ If you enter the WJEC course at a school or college in Wales, you will be following either the England or the Wales option below.
♣ If you enter in England, you will be following the England option below.

Speaking & Listening (20% of the assessment)

♣ Speaking & Listening is assessed throughout your one-year or two-year course, with all candidates required to complete a range of activities.

English coursework *Wales option*	**English coursework** *England option*
1. Reading: Welsh relevance	1. Reading: Shakespeare play
2. Reading: Different cultures	2. Reading: Different cultures poetry
3. Writing: Narrative/expressive	3. Writing: Narrative/expressive
4. Writing: Analytical/persuasive	4. Writing: Analytical/persuasive
One piece must be teacher supervised. *One Reading piece must be Poetry.* *One Reading piece must be Drama.* *One piece at least must be handwritten.*	*One piece must be teacher supervised.* *One piece at least must be handwritten.*

English – Speaking & Listening
1. Group discussion and interaction
2. Individual extended contribution
3. Drama focused activity

ENGLISH PAPER 1 – Foundation and Higher tiers

Two hours (30% of the assessment)

> **Section A** (about 55 minutes recommended)
> **Reading:** Answer questions on a prose extract.
> *Questions test: knowledge and use of text; inference and interpretation; appreciation of language and structure.*
> **See pages 6–11 and 12–17 of this Revision Guide.**

> **Section B** (about 1 hour 5 minutes recommended)
> **Writing:** Complete two pieces of writing – descriptive and imaginative writing.
> *Writing assessed on: content and organisation; sentence structure, punctuation and spelling.* **See pages 18–24 of this Revision Guide.**

ENGLISH PAPER 2 – Foundation and Higher tiers

Two hours (30% of the assessment)

> **Section A** (about 50 minutes recommended)
> **Reading:** Answer questions on a non-fiction text and a media text.
> *Questions test: knowledge and use of text, including cross-referencing; inference, interpretation and evaluation of language structure and presentation.*
> **See pages 25–31 and 32–39 of this Revision Guide.**

> **Section B** (about 1 hour 10 minutes recommended)
> **Writing:** Complete two pieces of writing – transactional and discursive writing.
> *Writing assessed on: content and organisation; sentence structure, punctuation and spelling.* **See pages 40–47 of this Revision Guide.**

PAPER 1 SECTION A – LITERARY PROSE READING
FOUNDATION TIER
Text from *The Rainbow* by D.H. Lawrence (novel)

Ursula is a young, untrained teacher who is starting her first job in a small mining town in England at the start of the 20th century.

She dreamed how she would make the little, ugly children love her. She would be so *personal*. Teachers were always so hard and impersonal. There was no vivid relationship. She would make everything personal and vivid, she would give herself, she would give, give, give all her great stores of wealth to her children, she would make them *so* happy, and they would prefer her to any teacher on the face of the earth. 5

At Christmas she would choose such fascinating Christmas cards for them, and she would give them such a happy party in one of the classrooms.

The head-master, Mr Harby, was a short, thick-set, rather common man, she thought. But she would hold before him the light of grace and refinement, he would have her in such high esteem, before long; she would be the gleaming sun of the school, the children would 10 blossom like little weeds, the teachers like tall, hard plants would burst into rare flower.

*

Ursula faced her class, some fifty-five boys and girls who stood filling the ranks of the desks. She felt utterly non-existent. She had no place nor being there. She faced the block of children.

Down the room she heard the rapid firing of questions. She stood before her class not 15 knowing what to do. She waited painfully. Her block of children, fifty unknown faces, watched her, hostile, ready to jeer. She felt as if she were in torture over a fire of faces.

*

Of unutterable length and torture the seconds went by.

Then she gathered courage. She heard Mr Brunt asking questions in mental arithmetic. She stood near to her class, so that her voice need not be raised too much, and faltering, 20 uncertain, she said:

'Seven hats at two-pence ha'penny each?'

A grin went over the faces of the class, seeing her commence. She was red and suffering. Then some hands shot up like blades, and she asked for the answer.

The day passed incredibly slowly. She never knew what to do, there came horrible gaps, 25 when she was merely exposed to the children; and when, relying on some pert little girl for information, she had started a lesson, she did not know how to go on with it properly. The children were her masters.

*

The first week passed in a blind confusion. She did not know how to teach, and she felt she would never know. Mr Harby came down every now and again to her class, to see 30 what she was doing. She felt so incompetent as he stood by, bullying and threatening, so unreal, that she wavered, became neutral and non-existent. But he stood there watching with that listening-genial smile of the eyes, that was really threatening; he said nothing, he made her go on teaching, she felt she had no soul in her body. Then he went away, and his going was like a derision. The class was his class. She was a wavering substitute. He 35 thrashed and bullied, he was hated. But he was master. Though she was gentle and always considerate of her class, yet they belonged to Mr Harby, and they did not belong to her.

*

She went on rather doggedly, blindly, waiting for a crisis. Mr Harby had now begun to persecute her. Her dread and hatred of him grew and loomed larger and larger. She was afraid he was going to bully her and destroy her. He began to persecute her because she could not keep her class in proper condition, because her class was the weak link in the chain which made up the school.

*

Every now and again Mr Harby would swoop down to examine exercise books. For a whole hour, he would be going round the class, taking book after book, comparing page after page, whilst Ursula stood aside for all the remarks and fault-finding to be pointed at her through the scholars. It was true, since she had come, the composition books had grown more and more untidy, disorderly, filthy. Mr. Harby pointed to the pages done before her regime, and to those done after, and fell into a passion of rage. Many children he sent out to the front with their books. And after he had thoroughly gone through the silent and quivering class, he caned the worst offenders well, in front of the others, thundering in real passion of anger and chagrin.

*

Then came another infliction. There were not enough pens to go round the class. She sent to Mr Harby for more. He came in person.

'Not enough pens, Miss Brangwen?' he said, with the smile and calm of exceeding rage against her.

'No, we are six short,' she said, quaking.

'Oh, how is that?' he said, menacingly. Then, looking over the class, he asked:

'How many are there here to-day?'

'Fifty-two,' said Ursula, but he did not take any notice, counting for himself.

'Fifty-two,' he said, 'And how many pens are there, Staples?'

Ursula was now silent. He would not heed her if she answered, since he had addressed the monitor.

'That's a very curious thing,' said Mr Harby, looking over the silent class with a slight grin of fury. All the childish faces looked up at him blank and exposed.

'A few days ago,' the master went on, 'there were sixty pens for this class – now there are forty-eight. What is forty-eight from sixty, Williams?' There was a sinister suspense in the question. A thin, ferret-faced boy in a sailor suit started up exaggeratedly.

'Please, Sir!' he said. Then a slow, sly grin came over his face. He did not know. There was a tense silence. The boy dropped his head. Then he looked up again, a little cunning triumph in his eyes. 'Twelve,' he said.

'I would advise you to attend,' said the head-master dangerously. The boy sat down.

'Forty-eight from sixty is twelve: so there are twelve pens to account for. Have you looked for them, Staples?'

'Yes, Sir.'

'Then look again.'

The scene dragged on. Two pens were found: ten were missing. Then the storm burst.

'Am I to have you thieving, besides your dirt and bad work and bad behaviour?' the head-master began. 'Not content with being the worst-behaved and dirtiest class in the school, you are thieves into the bargain, are you? It is a very funny thing! Pens don't melt into the air: pens are not in the habit of mizzling away into nothing. What has become of them? For they must be found, and found by Standard Five. They were lost by Standard Five, and they must be found.'

Ursula stood and listened, her heart hard and cold. She was so much upset, that she felt almost mad. Something in her tempted her to turn on the head-master and tell him to stop, about the miserable pens. But she did not. She could not.

40

45

50

55

60

65

70

75

80

85

Reading and response

Answer the following questions.

A1. **Read lines 1 – 11**
What do you find out about Ursula in these lines? [5]

A2. **Read lines 12 – 28**
What evidence is there to suggest that Ursula is unprepared for teaching? [5]

A3. **Read lines 29 – 51**
What do you think of the way that Mr Harby behaves towards Ursula?
Refer closely to the text in your answer. [10]

A4. **Read from line 52 to the end of the passage**
How does the writer make these lines tense and dramatic? [10]
Consider:
- how Ursula feels
- how the children behave
- how Mr Harby behaves
- the words the writer chooses.

A5. **Now consider the passage as a whole.**
Imagine you are Ursula.
Write a letter to a friend about your experiences as a teacher.
Remember this is a test of your understanding. Your answer must be based on
the passage. [10]

———————————————— **Tips before you start** ————————————————

In this section of Paper 1 you will have to read and answer questions on an extract of a novel or short story written by a well-established writer of the 20th century. Expect some difficult words and phrases; learn how to deal with them without panicking. Concentrate on what you understand, rather than on what you do not understand.

*Take about 55 minutes for this section of the exam. Expect most of the questions to be worth 10 marks and try to make your answers at least half a side of A4 long. Answers to questions worth 5 marks should obviously be shorter: either a list of five items or a paragraph of about three or four sentences. Always give yourself a chance to score high marks. Above all, don't miss out any questions and answer **all** of them to their full value. Make sure you concentrate each time on the correct lines of the text.*

A1. Try to write a clear answer that includes the straightforward things about Ursula in the first ten lines. Look for five points, though you may well pick up the marks here more quickly if you make interesting comments about Ursula that show you can read between the lines. Do not write too much – this question is worth 5 marks, not 10.

A2. This is also worth 5 marks, not 10. It asks for 'evidence', so it is reasonable to expect that five pieces of evidence are needed for full marks. The question does **not** ask you to explain why you have chosen the points, so do not waste your time.

A3. This question focuses particularly on Mr Harby, but on Ursula too. It asks your opinion on the way he behaves towards her, so you are expected to have a view and to back it up with sensible reasoning. You may believe he is fair towards her or you may think that he is unfair – it doesn't matter which, but you should be able to argue a case. You may be able to extend an answer by thoughtfully considering different points of view, but do not hang around too long on this question, because there are still two to go in this section. This answer should be longer than either of the previous two.

A4. This question is possibly the hardest in the section, because it is a 'How...?' question which focuses on the way the writer has written a part of the passage. Concentrate on the key word 'tense' and try to explain what is dramatic and gripping about this particular scene in the classroom. Lawrence brings a tense situation to life – try to represent it fairly by saying not only **what** happens in the scene but **how** it happens.

A5. There is always the possibility of an empathy question – one which requires you to 'play the part' of a character and to invent their words. Do **not** begin your answer with 'If I were Ursula, I would say that I was...'. From the very start, place yourself deep into her situation and write her thoughts and feelings directly. This too is a test of understanding, so write in a way that focuses on the events of the passage.

Exploring responses

A1. Ursula imagines that 'she would be so personal' while teaching the children, getting to know them properly, in comparison to other teachers who are 'always so hard and impersonal'. She imagines that she would be really popular with the children, 'they would prefer her to any teacher on the face on the earth', because she is generous and 'she would give, give, give...' Ursula also seems to believe that she is unique and special – more special than the other members of staff, 'she would be the gleaming sun of the school'. She seems keen, but very naïve.

The examiner is expecting you to pick out key things about Ursula from the first ten lines, but also, if possible, to show that you clearly and deeply understand the points that you are choosing. If you make a few straight-forward points, plus at least one confident moment of 'reading between the lines', you earn full marks.

A2. She felt really bad in front of the class. She stands 'before her class not knowing what to do'. Her voice is also 'faltering, uncertain' when she first speaks to the class. She showed her lack of planning because 'when...she had started a lesson, she did not know how to go on with it properly'. She was embarrassed and red in the face. She had to rely on the children to give her information and there were gaps in her lessons.

Five clear points of evidence would probably earn you full marks here and you could even present them in a list to be efficient. Don't worry if you say things slightly differently, provided you try to make distinct points. Do not waste time explaining your evidence if the question does not require it.

A3. Mr Harby threatens and intimidates Ursula during her lessons, but it is because Ursula is nervous about her teaching. Mr Harby physically does very little in Ursula's lessons, 'he said nothing, he made her go on teaching'. However, although he does very little, 'he stood there watching', she feels threatened by his presence. Ursula believes that Mr Harby is thinking that she is a hopeless teacher but Mr Harby does not actually tell her this. Ursula is 'afraid he was going to bully her and destroy her,' but maybe this is not Mr Harby's aim. In fact Ursula herself admits that 'her class was the weak link in the chain which made up the school' and that 'she could not keep her class in proper condition'. Mr Harby's behaviour seems unfair but Ursula even admits herself that she is not a very good teacher, 'since she had come, the composition books had grown more and more untidy, disorderly, filthy'. Mr Harby has every right to be angry about this. However, when he 'fell into a passion of rage' he took his anger out on the children; he sent many to the front of the class and 'caned the worst offenders'. Although he reprimands these children 'in front of the others', he does not reprimand Ursula. I think Mr Harby understands that Ursula has a difficult class, perhaps the worst in the school, and he tries to offer his support to her but she misinterprets this. Therefore, although Mr Harby at first seems like a bully towards Ursula, this is explained only from Ursula's biased point of view.

It is clear that Mr Harby is not the most sensitive of people and he does not appear to support Ursula. However, opinions may vary as to whether he behaves very badly towards her. Whatever your thoughts, make sure you focus on the relationship between the two of them. Do not write about one of the characters without reference to the other. The above answer is very thoughtful and is the product of a close reading.

A4. Things are already quite tense, but this part of the passage opens with 'then came another infliction'. This warns the reader that something is about to happen. It makes the reader feel impatient to find out what will happen. The reader also feels nervous for Ursula, because it is hard to believe that things can get much worse for her. The reader will feel tense because instead of Mr Harby simply sending down a box of pens for Ursula he comes to see the class in person. He enters Ursula's class 'with the smile and calm of exceeding rage against her'. This creates the impression that Mr Harby is trying to control his temper but it builds tension because the reader knows he will soon explode with anger. Ursula says very little to Mr Harby; she answers his questions with very short statements and then says nothing when she thinks that he is not taking any notice of her. This makes the reader feel frustrated because as these events unfold Ursula becomes more and more frozen with fear, despite the fact that the reader is willing her to do something – anything.

The class is described as looking 'blank and exposed', making the reader feel sorry for them; they are the victims. There is a contrast between Mr Harby's anger and rage and everyone else's terrified silence. This event takes a painfully long time to reach its climax. Everyone seems to be feeling how slowly this episode is passing, 'The scene dragged on'. Even after this, only 'Two pens were found', meaning that the agony has to be drawn out even further. The reader feels so uncomfortable reading this and it is almost a relief when finally 'the storm burst' and Mr Harby gives full vent to his anger.

Even as the passage ends, the reader feels tense. Once again, the reader's attention is drawn to Ursula. She is feeling 'so much upset' and the reader thinks that she will do something to prevent the headmaster from continuing his tirade. This moment is very tense as 'something in her tempted her to turn on the head-master and tell him to stop'. However, much to the relief of the reader, 'But she did not. She could not'. Finally, the reader can relax – Ursula will not do anything.

You can follow the bullet points or you can track the text for a question like this one. There is much to say and you can respond personally as an engaged reader as well as more technically as a student. This is a well sustained and well organised answer.

A5.

Dear _____

I have had a terrible week teaching. As you know I had such wonderful visions about how teaching would be. I thought I would be so personal. All of the children would love me and I would give them everything. They would even have cards and parties at Christmas. It was going to be wonderful. I even thought that the school would love me. My colleagues would all say how I was the gleaming sun of the school and how much I have improved things since I started.

How wrong I was. Things could not have been more different. Instead of the gleaming sun I feel like a storm and I feel like I have ruined everything good about the class I teach.

On my first day I was faced with fifty boys and girls in Standard Five. They faced me like some terrible army, waiting to attack at the first sign of weakness. I felt completely non-existent. Like I would never have control over my class. I was frozen into silence, incapable of uttering a single syllable to them. The seconds crawled by and still I had not spoken to them. Even once I'd started there were still huge gaps in my lessons. I felt exposed to the children, like they knew that I really had no idea what I was doing. It felt like they were my masters and I had to obey them.

The head-master, Mr Harby, has been the worst of it all though. At the beginning he merely came into my class and stood there saying nothing. Just seeing him in my class I knew that he didn't think I was capable of teaching. All the time it felt like he was bullying me and threatening me even without saying a word. I really don't understand it. He thrashes the children and bullies them; I am nothing but kind and personal and instead they respect him and obey him and not me. It only got worse and worse. Mr Harby began examining their books and I know they've become so much more untidy and disorderly since I began teaching here. He took individual children — the worst offenders — up to the front of the class and punished them with the cane. To cap it all, he launched a major investigation about some lost pens and I had to stand in silence, humiliated, while he sorted out things again.

Please write soon to cheer me up and advise me what to do. I can only hope that things improve next week, though I doubt it.

Best wishes,
Ursula

A strong empathy response, like this one, must reflect understanding of the events of the text, but also recreate the character successfully. There is scope for making Ursula depressed or defiant or both, but empathy work must, by definition, have some convincing feeling. This response shows thorough understanding, and is sensitive too.

HIGHER TIER

Text from *The Remains of the Day* by Kazuo Ishiguro (novel)

Stevens, the butler at Dartington Hall, a great English country house in the middle years of the 20th century, describes an occasion when Miss Kenton, the housekeeper, brings a vase of flowers to his hideaway, the butler's pantry.

The butler's pantry, as far as I am concerned, is a crucial office, the heart of the house's operations, not unlike a general's headquarters during a battle and it is imperative that all things in it are ordered — and left ordered — in precisely the way I wish them to be. I have never been that sort of butler who allows all sorts of people to wander in and out with their queries and grumbles. If operations are to be conducted in a smoothly co-ordinated way, it is surely obvious that the butler's pantry must be the one place in the house where privacy and solitude are guaranteed.

As it happened, when she entered my pantry that evening, I was not in fact engaged in professional matters. That is to say, it was towards the end of the day during a quiet week and I had been enjoying a rare hour or so off duty. As I say, I am not certain if Miss Kenton entered with her vase of flowers, but I certainly do recall her saying:

"Mr Stevens, your room looks even less accommodating at night than it does in the day. The electric bulb is too dim, surely, for you to be reading by."

"It is perfectly adequate, thank you, Miss Kenton."

"Really, Mr Stevens, this room resembles a prison cell. All one needs is a small bed in the corner and one could well imagine condemned men spending their last hours here."

Perhaps I said something to this, I do not know. In any case, I did not look up from my reading, and a few moments passed during which I waited for Miss Kenton to excuse herself and leave. But then I heard her say:

"Now I wonder what it could be you are reading there, Mr Stevens."

"Simply a book, Miss Kenton."

"I can see that, Mr Stevens. But what sort of book — that is what interests me."

I looked up to see Miss Kenton advancing towards me. I shut the book, and clutching it to my person, rose to my feet.

"Really, Miss Kenton," I said, "I must ask you to respect my privacy."

"But why are you so shy about your book, Mr Stevens? I rather suspect it may be something rather racy."

"It is quite out of the question, Miss Kenton, that anything 'racy' as you put it, should be found on his lordship's shelves."

"I have heard it said that many learned books contain the most racy of passages, but I have never had the nerve to look. Now, Mr Stevens, do please allow me to see what it is you are reading."

"Miss Kenton, I must ask you to leave me alone. It is quite impossible that you should persist in pursuing me like this during the very few moments of spare time I have to myself."

But Miss Kenton was continuing to advance and I must say it was a little difficult to assess what my best course of action would be. I was tempted to thrust the book into the drawer of my desk and lock it, but this seemed absurdly dramatic. I took a few paces back, the book still held to my chest.

"Please show me the volume you are holding, Mr Stevens," Miss Kenton said, continuing her advance, "and I will leave you to the pleasures of your reading. What on earth can it be you are so anxious to hide?" 45

"Miss Kenton, whether or not you discover the title of this volume is in itself not of the slightest importance to me. But as a matter of principle, I object to your appearing like this and invading my private moments."

"I wonder, is it a perfectly respectable volume, Mr Stevens, or are you in fact protecting me from its shocking influences?" 50

Then she was standing before me, and suddenly the atmosphere underwent a peculiar change — almost as though the two of us had been suddenly thrust on to some other plane of being altogether. I am afraid it is not easy to describe clearly what I mean here. All I can say is that everything around us suddenly became very still; it was my impression that Miss Kenton's manner also underwent a sudden 55 change; there was a strange seriousness in her expression, and it struck me she seemed almost frightened.

"Please, Mr Stevens, let me see your book."

She reached forward and began gently to release the volume from my grasp. I judged it best to look away while she did so, but with her person positioned so 60 closely, this could only be achieved by my twisting my head away at a somewhat unnatural angle. Miss Kenton continued very gently to prise the book away, practically one finger at a time. The process seemed to take a very long time — throughout which I managed to maintain my posture — until I finally heard her say:

"Good gracious, Mr Stevens, it isn't anything so scandalous at all. Simply a 65 sentimental love story."

I believe it was around this point that I decided there was no need to tolerate any more. I cannot recall precisely what I said, but I remember showing Miss Kenton out of my pantry quite firmly and the episode was thus brought to a close.

Reading and response

Answer the following questions.

A1. **Read lines 1 – 26**
What are your impressions of Stevens in these lines? How does the writer create these impressions? [10]

A2. **Read lines 27 – 49**
How does the writer try to make these lines amusing? [10]

A3. **Read from line 50 to the end of the passage**
How do you react to the relationship between Stevens and Miss Kenton?
Why do you react as you do?
Refer closely to the text in your answer. [10]

A4. **Now consider the passage as a whole.**
How does the writer reveal Stevens' character and attitudes? [10]
Consider:
- the way Stevens speaks and behaves in the story
- the way Stevens tells the story
- the way the writer structures the story.

————————————— Tips before you start —————————————

Higher tier questions in this section of Paper 1 will consistently focus on the writer's skills and techniques. As in the equivalent part of the Foundation tier, the section will test students' understanding of a prose passage from an established literary figure. Timings throughout the papers are the same for the Higher tier as for the Foundation tier, so take about 55 minutes to answer these questions. There will be four questions worth 10 marks each on the Higher tier, so give each of them between 10 and 15 minutes of your time after you have read the passage initially.

A1. The first half of this question encourages your personal response, while the second half expects you to support it with evidence from the text. Your answer will be marked on its overall quality, not in two halves, but make sure you do not ignore the second part.

A2. Humour is quite difficult to explain, so some thought must be given to the details in the lines indicated. You need to picture the scene as described, as well as 'hear' the words that the characters speak and the way that they speak. Do not write off the humour because it does not instantly make you laugh out loud – think in terms of amusing, rather than hilarious.

A3. This question asks you to consider both characters, not especially as individuals, but as they appear to relate to each other. There is an element of personal response required here again, and you need to be able to explain your views persuasively, using the subtleties of the text to back up your opinions.

A4. The final question places some importance on your ability to select and highlight effectively from the text, and to be able to understand how the writer creates and develops a character and organises a 'scene'. Remember that Stevens is telling the story, looking back at an incident in which he himself was one of the two characters involved.

———————

Exploring responses

A1. *First impressions of Mr Stevens are that he is a very serious man. His language is full of military imagery as if he likens himself to an army general, possibly implying that he believes his role to be as important as Nelson's! He believes his quarters are "not unlike a general's headquarters during a battle". There is a self-importance about him.*

He makes little or no effort to engage Miss Kenton in conversation when she enters his room, "I waited for Miss Kenton to excuse herself and leave". He is polite, but clearly uninterested in making unnecessary conversation, and in response to one of Miss Kenton's queries he merely adds, "Perhaps I said something to this, I do not know". This makes him seem cold and unfriendly towards her attempts at engaging him in a conversation. Throughout this scene he speaks to Miss Kenton in brief, succinct statements, asking her no questions and limiting his responses to as few words as possible.

The conversation is very formal and Stevens appears to hide behind the formality to keep his privacy. At the opening of the passage he is "enjoying a rare hour or so off duty", suggesting that he finds it difficult to find any time to himself and that his position as butler keeps him very busy.

He likes his privacy and isolation away from the rest of the house, "the butler's pantry must be the one place in the house where privacy and solitude are guaranteed". He knows his place, but he has an air of superiority too. He does seem satisfied though with the bare necessities of life, his room appearing to "resemble a prison cell". He is obviously a very private man — "I must ask you to respect my privacy." — and he wants to bring the conversation to an end by dismissing Miss Kenton from the room.

For an opening question, you are entitled to respond in a tentative way, reflecting the fact that your wider understanding of a character is not yet developed. You need to go carefully and not gamble with loose speculations, but the comparison between being a butler and a military general is a gift to a sound candidate. Understanding the formality of the language is crucial for a secure mark. Overall here, the answer is thorough, perceptive and subtle.

A2. In this section, Miss Kenton teases Mr Stevens about the book he is reading. She is being playful but he seems to become more and more flustered by her teasing, and tries in vain to maintain his dignity. The lines almost entirely consist of dialogue, so there is a strong sense of comic drama as you can 'hear' and 'see' Stevens' unease at the close presence of a woman!

The reader finds it humorous because it is a chase scene, with Miss Kenton pursuing Mr Stevens. In the previous passage Stevens appeared pompous and serious, but here he gradually becomes more and more flustered with Miss Kenton's questioning. This change in Stevens is obviously funny to the reader. Miss Kenton firstly teases him that the novel he is reading is "racy", not very respectable, and carries on suggestively about his choice.

Mr Stevens becomes increasingly flustered and he protests, "Miss Kenton, I must ask you to leave". This is clearly humorous because of the role reversal. In most typical cases, it would be the woman who feels threatened by the presence of the man and would ask him to leave. This is funny as well because it is a stark contrast to the start of the passage.

Stevens realises that he is losing this battle and begins to panic, though he understates this amusingly, "I must say it was a little difficult to assess what my best course of action would be". His panic becomes more evident and the reader would agree that his suggestion to "thrust the book into the drawer of my desk" is indeed "absurdly dramatic". The reader realises that Stevens is effectively cornered by Miss Kenton and can only resort to bargaining and appealing to her to try and get her to leave his office, "I object to your appearing like this and invading my private moments". His words here do not match his actions or his thoughts at all, "whether or not you discover the title of this volume is in itself not of the slightest importance to me". The reader would recognise the irony of the statement and would find this funny. If this were true, then why is Stevens making such a fuss? Miss Kenton has the final word in this section, "are you in fact protecting me from its shocking influences?" She has maintained control of the situation from the beginning and the reader would find it funny that even up until the last moment she continues mocking him. He dramatically over reacts and his previously calm and serious attitude has been replaced by a flustered embarrassed mess. This is even funnier when considering that this dramatic change has occurred simply because of the book he is reading. It is a simple meeting that is presented as farce.

Although you are entitled to lose your sense of humour during a period of exams, you ought to see some potential comedy in this passage. There is a build-up of evidence that shows that Stevens is wriggling under pressure in a comic way, so try to let your enjoyment of the extract show through a little. Remember the question and apply the right kind of vocabulary to signal the humour.

A3. Stevens does not make it very clear what is going on in these lines between him and Miss Kenton, probably because he doesn't really understand it himself. It appears that the atmosphere changes suddenly and that there is a potentially romantic moment as they find themselves close to each other. Miss Kenton perhaps realises it is the moment of truth and she is not frightened, as Stevens guesses, but in a state of anticipation that Stevens will drop his guard and fall for her! But he doesn't appear to have any of the instincts that she is expecting, even when she touches his hands and tries 'gently to prise the book away'. The drama is described in intricate detail 'practically one finger at a time' and we are encouraged to believe that time stood still. The spell is broken finally because Stevens and Miss Kenton are on completely different wavelengths — as Miss Kenton tries to become more and more personal and informal, Stevens retreats behind proper behaviour ("I managed to maintain my posture" and "showing Miss Kenton out of my pantry quite firmly"). It is hard to think of anyone being as naïve as Stevens these days and it is laughable to us that they even called each other by their formal names. This made it very difficult for Miss Kenton to show her feelings and Stevens was maybe even in denial of his.

Miss Kenton's teasing of Stevens can be seen as playful and she obviously feels affection for him. It is also highly likely that Stevens is attracted to Miss Kenton. He becomes flustered and embarrassed when she tries to take the book off him, "I judged it best to look away while she did so, but...this could only be achieved by my twisting my head away at a somewhat unnatural angle". His embarrassment may be because he believes his feelings towards Miss Kenton are inappropriate or it could be that as yet he simply doesn't realise that he is attracted to her.

This is obviously a painful situation for Stevens, "The process seemed to take a very long time". It is obvious that Stevens has not had a lot of close contact with women on this personal level. He creates the impression that he likes to maintain a professional distance and this makes his relationship with Miss Kenton seem really awkward. The fact that the incident is told from Stevens' point of view affects the way the reader interprets it. Although the narrative seems to be very frank, "it struck me she seemed almost frightened", the reader does not really get any information about the way Miss Kenton feels about the situation.

It is not easy when you have to interpret a passage through an 'unreliable narrator', in this case Stevens, who is a complex character. You can generalise successfully about a relationship, but many comments may be about two distinct halves. It is critical, too, that directly or implicitly, you show a sense of understanding the quaint inhibitions of a bygone age.

A4. Stevens' character and attitudes come to the reader directly from Stevens himself. In other words, the writer presents Stevens as the first-person narrator and it is solely from his point of view that we get the story. The passage contains mainly dialogue, but it is all from the 'memory' of Stevens, who has a particular slant on things. Miss Kenton's words and actions reveal a great deal indirectly about Stevens, however, because she challenges him and allows us to see beyond his skin-deep character.

It is a very tightly narrated incident, because from beginning to end it covers a time-span of only a few minutes at most. Stevens appears at first to be a commanding authority figure, but soon he is seriously ruffled by an innocent event, before regaining his composure to resume his normal character. As the narrator, Stevens tries to be faithful to his memory, recounting fully and in detail the words and actions as he remembers them. He does not seem capable of much reflection or self-awareness.

Stevens' language is very formal, in keeping with his character. He has a leisurely, eloquent style, which reflects the class and style of an English country home. He can also assert himself firmly – 'I must ask you...', 'It is quite out of the question...', 'I object...'. He is only the butler, but he has to mix with the toffs, so he cannot allow his language to slip anywhere near dialect, slang or even plain English. All in all he represents the stiff upper lip of the traditional Englishman, but his behaviour in this incident suggests that he is emotionally underdeveloped.

This question invites an answer that shows overall understanding of the passage through explanation of structure and style, and rather less word/phrase detail than some other questions might prompt. An observation that the extract is dominated by dialogue obviously does not need an example of dialogue to prove it. Certain points can be general, but they should not be vague - if a comment is so loose that it could apply equally to almost all texts, then it will be of little value. Respond to the effects of the words, phrases and sentences that are on the page in front of you.

BE AWARE!

In Paper 1 Section A of both tiers, the skills of LITERARY PROSE READING include:
- Locating points in the texts
- Using your own words to show understanding
- Reading between the lines
- Empathising with characters
- Appreciating the skills of writers

DO
read the text closely and respond sensitively

DO NOT
use technical terms that you don't understand

PAPER 1 SECTION B – DESCRIPTIVE AND IMAGINATIVE WRITING
Writing to *inform, explain, describe* and writing to *explore, imagine, entertain.*
FOUNDATION / HIGHER TIER

This section of the exam is common to both tiers – the tasks will be the same for both tiers.

Descriptive writing task

B1.   Describe the scene in a school or college classroom at the end of the day.   [20]

You should not need to write more than a page in your [A4] answer book.

Remember that this is a test of your ability to write descriptively.

——————————————— **Tips before you start** ———————————————

*The descriptive writing task requires a 'picture in words'. It does NOT call for the action
of a story, but you do need some variety of observation, some movement, some
individuality for a successful piece of writing. From the first word to last in this short
piece of writing, stay with the place you are describing.*

*You may be looking at the classroom through the eyes of an outsider or someone inside the
room. Capture the moment at the end of the day, when pupils are about to leave or have
just left. The room may be empty of people or there may be one or more people still inside.*

Choose your words thoughtfully and write your sentences with care.

Remember: this is descriptive writing, not narrative writing. **Do not write a story.**

———————————————

Exploring responses: a classroom scene

B1.   *Alone in the corner of the classroom the teacher slumps down into his
chair, breathing a heavy sigh of relief. He sits staring around at the
mess and chaos left by thirty boys and girls who have just run noisily
and happily out of the school building at the end of the day. Who would
have thought that eight-year-olds could be so untidy? The weary
teacher loosens his tie and begins the job of gathering his papers
together from his desk.*

   *The room really does look like a bomb has hit it. Not a single chair
is neatly under its desk. Coloured pencils and crayons lie crazily all over
the desks and on one desk there is an enormous splatter of
multicoloured paint. The teacher's eyes pause over this mess and he
sighs again; the cleaners will go mad when they see the paint spilled
everywhere. He grabs a handful of paper towels from a shelf in the
classroom and tries to mop up some of the spill. At first it only seems
to be making things worse, but he keeps trying.*

   *Looking down, he sees bits of broken biros lying on the floor of the
classroom, carelessly stamped on by tiny feet. Crumpled balls of paper
lie like snowballs; the product of a paper fight by the looks of it. "How
difficult is it to put the rubbish in the bin?" he thinks to himself; but
looking round he sees that the bin is already overflowing with litter.
Under one desk there is a tiny pile of sweet wrappers, where two of the
pupils had obviously been munching on Starbursts during the lessons.
The floor is covered in tiny round pieces of confetti; where some child was
careless with the hole punch and all the circles of paper had fallen out.*

   *Leaves, acorns and pine cones from the Nature Table lie on the floor
underneath it or dangle off the edge. Not even the goldfish tank has*

managed to avoid the chaos. A pencil bobs in the water, occasionally nudged by the curious nose of the goldfish who mouths his protests at the teacher.

The teacher, exhausted from his long day, collects his pile of papers and heads for the door. He looks back as he puts his hand on the door knob, knowing that all the mess and chaos will magically be tidied by the cleaners overnight, ready for the children to come to school tomorrow and wreak havoc all over again.

A large amount of imagination goes into a piece of descriptive writing. Decisions are made – here is a teacher (male) in a classroom (primary) which is entirely empty of pupils. The room is, not unexpectedly, in a mess at the end of the day. The classroom is brought to life, however, by the details of description imaginatively chosen, the loosening of the tie, the Starbursts, the acorns and pine cones, the goldfish tank. The sentences are controlled and varied, and the piece is shaped finally by the sense of the cleaners working to prepare the room for another day. The writing is deliberate and precise, but not beyond the careful construction of someone with a sound, developing command of language.

BE AWARE!

In Paper 1 Section B of both tiers, the skills of DESCRIPTIVE WRITING include:
- Focus on detail
- Organisation of content
- Accuracy of language

DO
write naturally about a scene that you can see in your mind

DO NOT
write a story

Imaginative writing task

B2. Choose **one** of the following titles for your writing. [20]

The quality of your writing is more important than its length. As a guide, write about two pages in your [A4] answer book.

Either (a) The Best Christmas I Ever Had

or (b) Write a story based on the feeling of jealousy

or (c) Continue the following:
'I had never liked mobile phones...'

or (d) The Accident

or (e) Write a story which ends with these words:
'...and I walked off with my head held high.'

———————————————— **Tips before you start** ————————————————

You should be able to make a positive choice from the five 'titles' on offer. It is surely worth taking a few minutes to decide which is the best one for you. For most students, it is best to keep within the bounds of realism when you are writing a narrative. In other words, write a story reasonably within the scope of your personal experience – even if it is not something that has actually happened to you. Some people do thrive on fantasy or science fiction or horror, but generally it is a good idea for most students to avoid 'genres' like these.

You are writing a 'short story' but it is not going to be 30 or 40 pages long, like most published versions. You need to work out your 'coverage' – the time-span, the characters, the setting for the story. You cannot easily go halfway round the world and back in not much more than two pages of writing! Think of how you are going to end your story, just as you must think about how you will begin it. Then you will have a chance of managing the steps along the way, which may have to be quite limited. Save your novel for another day!

Organisation and accuracy are the key qualities of both imaginative and descriptive writing. This means paying close attention to: paragraphing, sentence structure, grammar, punctuation and spelling. If you have a cool head, you will remember paragraphs, you will control and vary your sentences with proper punctuation and you will make only limited 'word' errors of grammar and spelling. If you rush and panic, your work will lose its shape and your key skills will be in disarray.

————————————————

Exploring responses: from autobiography to fiction

The following three pieces of writing show different types of imaginative writing – responding personally with what appears to be genuine autobiography, borrowing from personal experience and everyday life to create a seemingly exaggerated narrative, and shaping a more self-consciously 'literary' narrative from a realistic, but potentially life-changing situation. Each one of these responses deserves high praise and reward. They are all convincingly constructed from first word to last and are precisely expressed in terms of spelling, punctuation and grammar.

B2. *The Best Christmas I Ever Had*

Back in 1964 I was just four years old, and I didn't understand the world. In my small mind, that Christmas morning was just like any other Christmas morning. However, it was when I noticed Daddy's worried look and heard Mammy's faint moans from upstairs that my small young body began to tense with a sense of grown up anxiety.

The brightly coloured parcels distracted my concerns and I ripped open the cheap paper with podgy, trembling fingers. My heart leapt with delight when those beautiful shoes fell into my lap. The perspex high heels and elastic straps were almost the same as I bought my daughter yesterday. Her face when she saw them, and the noise she made when she clacked across the parquet floor in our huge bungalow, brought all the memories to the front of my mind where they exploded like fireworks on November 5th. I remember taking off my bunny slippers and squashing my chubby feet down under the elastic. I stood up, balancing precariously in the heels, my nylon nightdress bristling with electricity and clinging to me. I climbed the step to the kitchen and click-clacked over to the back door. As I was about to open the door, I heard the front door open behind me and, when I turned, I saw a dark-haired, exotic woman, wearing a black cape, fly up the stairs followed closely by my Daddy. I wondered momentarily what was happening, but turned back to the beautiful shoes.

Out in the back yard my shoes made a different sound and I clomped to and fro, goosebumps on my arms and smokes of cold breath billowing from my mouth. I opened the outhouse door latch and climbed into the icy cold toilet. My warm urine splashed into the cold water and I kicked my feet higher so I could pee and admire my shoes at the same time. A spider was weaving his intricate web in the corner of the old brick building and it stretched all the way down to where the squares of newspaper were pierced by a rusty nail. I would, on other days, have paused to admire the fleecy web but today my shoes were needing to make noises.

As I click clacked back across the kitchen, Daddy appeared through the doorway holding a wriggling bundle of blankets. I walked over to him clumsily, aching for him to admire my new grown up shoes.

'Come here, bach,' said Daddy as he pulled the blanket down to reveal a red, squashed up face. 'Look, you have a new sister. Her name is Holly. Isn't this the best Christmas you've ever had?'

I looked at this strange creature with the tufts of jet black hair and spindly fists jabbing at the air, and I looked admiringly at my beautiful shoes.

'Yes,' I whispered contentedly, 'this is the best Christmas I've ever had.'

This is an excellent piece of autobiographical writing that recreates the mystery and charm of childhood. Briefly the writer adds another dimension, the extra reflection that comes from having a child of her own and witnessing an event that triggered the memories. The recall of feelings and visual details (and also the sound made by the shoes) is skilfully woven into the story. This particular student takes advantage of her own mature years to write about a distant memory in a complex way, but even a personal anecdote about a recent event could make a good piece of writing for students of any age. The process of looking back reflectively can still be effective even a short time after an event.

B2. <u>I had never liked mobile phones...</u>

I had never liked mobile phones and now I knew why. Two o'clock in the morning is never my most focused of times and the incessant shrill of my red handset, buried beneath a sea of bras, socks and skirts, wasn't exactly welcome. For several seconds my sleep-riddled mind couldn't place the sound, then I sneaked out a tentative arm from under the duvet and groped beneath my laundry.

"Yes?" I grunted. Amidst the static crackle of poor signal, I could hear laughter which I recognised immediately. "Did I wake you?" At the sound of his voice I felt my brain click into action. I smoothed my hair and wiped my tired eyes as though he could see me.

"It's two in the morning, on a Wednesday. Of course you woke me!" I replied, unable to keep the smile out of my voice. "But now I'm up, what's wrong?"

"Nothing..." I waited expectantly. "It's just..." I smiled knowledgeably. "Well, I need a favour."

"What kind of favour?" I said, propping the phone beneath my chin as I pulled on some clothes.

I paused in my dressing, eyebrows raised. "You see, I've done something, kind of...well, you'll see. Just meet me in the usual place." He hung up abruptly and I put the phone thoughtfully on the bed. That's what I loved about him, he was so unpredictable. A late night phone call wasn't unusual from him, he kept odd hours. A favour for him usually involved giving him a lift to whatever girl he was sleeping with at the time. I loved him, obviously, but to him I was just a friend. He had me exactly where he wanted me. I would do anything to please him, and he knew it.

He kissed me. Whenever we met he would kiss me to ensure that I remained enthralled. My cold numbed body suddenly tingled with warmth and a deep blush spread over my pale cheeks. "Hi," I said softly, unable to keep the quiver out of my voice. He smiled, assured, confident, perfect.

"Look at this," he whispered, motioning me to follow. Obediently I did.

Speechless I stood, gazing down into the ditch where he pointed. Numb again, but this time with shock, I turned to him. My eyes must have asked the question for he nodded and turned away.

"It wasn't my fault," he said softly. "I just thought you'd be sick of giving me lifts!"

Oh no, I thought, it's my fault. I knew it would be. Why can't I ever do anything right for him?

The crushed car lay embedded in the dirt, like a scar, a permanent reminder of my imperfections. I often felt like this around him. "What do you want me to do?" I murmured, sick with shame.

"Tell my dad it was you, he likes you. Oh yeah, also do you think that you could pay? Just until I get paid. I'll pay you back I promise."

Of course he wouldn't, I knew that. No, I decided, I'm sick of getting you out of trouble. You haven't passed your test, you shouldn't have been driving in the first place.

He smiled.

"Yeah, that's fine," I heard myself saying, inwardly cursing my weakness. Why do people get so stupid when they're in love? You'd think that someone would write a guide, telling you a sensible way to do it. All that I know is that, around him, I was weak.

He nodded. I always did what he told me and he knew it. Already he was on the phone, dialling Ashley or Abbie or whatever her name was.

"Yeah, it's sorted," he said to her. I bet that she didn't complain about being woken up either! He turned away, lowered his voice.

"Stupid cow, always does what I say."

The spell was broken. He didn't know I had heard, he thought I was waiting in the car to give him a lift.

I felt so angry. Once again, that numbness, only this time not to be dissipated by a kiss. Slowly I tapped him on the shoulder and, when he turned around, I threw his phone onto the ground and laughed in his face. I felt like I was fully awake for the first time in years, since I met him.

Returning to bed I saw my discarded mobile lying on the duvet. I smiled bitterly. I really do hate mobile phones...

This is a strong first-person narrative, probably fictional, but built around a sure-fire understanding of the way some people behave and the way some relationships work unequally. It revolves around a single incident within a short time-span, which is a large part of its effectiveness, because this narrative is about the immediate action of the girl on receiving the call, followed by her sudden change of attitude on the roadside shortly after. The narrative style, though very direct, also includes well-judged touches of visual and dramatic detail. The story's outcome will be very satisfying for most readers, for the girl has stood up for herself and broken free of the spell that belittled her.

B2. <u>The Accident</u>

She sat in the waiting room, clutching a cup of coffee. Her face was pale and her eyes looked tired. She was staring ahead of her as though she was in a trance. All around her, people were talking, babies were crying and in the distance, an ambulance siren could be heard. She didn't seem to notice.

'Mum, I'm going out!'

'Okay, don't be gone too long. I want you home in time for tea.'

She closed her eyes tightly and tried to shut out the memories. There was nothing she could have done, she told herself, but still the conversation replayed itself in her head. She felt like crying but she didn't have the strength. All she wanted was to be back at home, watching television with her precious little boy. No, she didn't, she thought. She wanted to talk to him, spend some time with him. She wanted to do something meaningful with him.

'Mrs Cooper?' a deep voice enquired.

She opened her eyes and looked up quickly.

'Yes, that's me,' she replied weakly.

'My name is Doctor Lowe. I've been treating your son. If you could follow me, I'll take you to his room.'

'Is he okay?' she asked anxiously. The doctor remained silent but, in his eyes, she could see sorrow. At once, her heart sank and as she stood up, she thought her knees might buckle. As they walked, the doctor explained her son's condition. She heard him, but she wasn't really listening. It was too much to take in. She heard the doctor say her son was in a stable condition, but he wasn't out of the woods yet. She nodded but she didn't make any eye contact. Finally he stopped and looked at her. The doctor was still young but his face had deep lines across the forehead. He had a kind, friendly face and a reassuring smile but his eyes spoke volumes. They gave away his thoughts but Mrs Cooper saw that he meant what he was saying.

'I will do everything I can for Adrian, so please don't give up hope,' he pleaded. 'He needs you.'

She nodded and blinked away her tears. Somehow she had to find strength, she told herself. Doctor Lowe showed her into the room.

'I'll give you some time alone,' he whispered.

The room was very small and various machines took up the space. A bed protruded into the middle of the room and on it lay her son. He was covered with a blanket but she could see all the wires and tubes hooked up to him. She walked slowly over to the bed and gasped when she saw his face. It was covered in cuts, bruises and stitches. It was a horrifying image and it stayed with her. She tried to recall how Adrian really looked, but all she could conjure up was how he looked now.

She took his hand and kissed it, resisting the urge to run out of the room. She wanted to talk to him but she wasn't quite sure what to say. She couldn't say something final, like goodbye, because she was still clinging on to the hope that he would recover. However, she didn't want to say anything trivial because she realised the gravity of the situation. Finally, she simply whispered 'I love you' and left silently.

She didn't go home that night. She couldn't. The thought of spending the night in an empty house away from Adrian terrified her. Instead, she accepted the nurse's offer to sleep in the family waiting room in the

Intensive Care Unit. Her sleep wasn't peaceful. It was haunted with images of Adrian's face and their last conversation. She dreamt of the moment Adrian stepped onto the road with the car speeding towards him. Several times in the night, she woke up in a cold sweat. Finally, she decided not to sleep and instead sat on a chair, looking out of the window and thinking of things like the shopping list and if she could afford to go on holiday next year. She thought about everything except Adrian, the accident and her terrifying nightmares.

A light knock on the door interrupted her thoughts. She looked up and saw Doctor Lowe enter. His face was grave and his deep eyes looked teary.

'No,' she thought. 'Please no.'

He opened his mouth to say the words she was dreading. Suddenly, he broke into a wide smile.

'He's awake.'

This student has chosen to interpret 'The Accident' as the consequences of an accident, focusing on the pain of the mother of the young victim, rather than the victim himself. It is a dramatic scene, narrated in the third person, with an opening of considerable impact. There is an intense build up that is maintained throughout until the tension is released by the unexpectedly happy twist at the end. It is presumably a fictional response to the title, but it has a powerful ring of truth. The thought processes of the boy's mother are utterly believable as she faces every parent's worst nightmare. The brief flashback to her last conversation with her son is effective, as are the two dialogues with the doctor. It is an extremely sensitive, understated piece of writing, which faces up to a tragic outcome even though the ending is one of great relief. The sentence control is especially precise – several of the sentences are very short – helping to create an extraordinary level of tension. The vocabulary is well-judged too, with key words exactly representing the seriousness of the situation.

BE AWARE!

In Paper 1 Section B of both tiers, the skills of IMAGINATIVE WRITING include:
- Control of a plot
- Development of character
- Attention to the opening and ending
- Using language for effect
- Control of punctuation

DO
plan your ending before you begin

DO NOT
dream up impossible stories

Texts: newspaper report and internet article

Read the following texts.

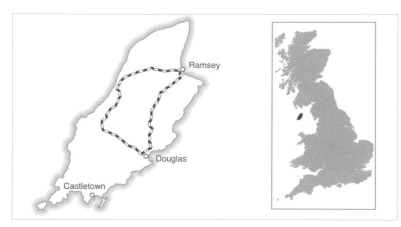

The TT (Tourist Trophy) professional motorbike races take place on the Isle of Man every summer and people visit the island from all over the world to see them. On the Sunday in the middle of the event, amateur motorcyclists are allowed to ride freely on the course around the island's roads.

The following newspaper report, 'An Open Road to Death', was printed in *The Times* newspaper on 8th June 2003. The article 'A Medic's TT 1994' was taken from the internet site of the Women's International Motorcycle Association (WIMA).

An Open Road To Death

Imagine a place where hundreds of motorbikes can race on public roads with absolutely no speed limit, and no need for special licences or training. For some it will sound like heaven, a dream opportunity to test their machines and reflexes without being hassled by the police. For others it will sound like a nightmare.

The surprise is that however far-fetched it might seem, it actually exists. Despite numerous deaths and growing controversy, it also has the full approval of the authorities.

Last weekend an estimated 40,000 people flocked to the Isle of Man for Mad Sunday, a day in the middle of the TT road race series in which anybody, however poorly trained, can get on the circuit and drive at speeds of up to 150mph.

Exciting as this might sound, nearly 200 people have been killed on this 37-mile circuit since the TT races began in 1907. So how wise can it be to allow novices to race without speed restrictions on roads with unforgiving obstacles such as telegraph poles, postboxes and sheer rock faces?

So what chance is there of an incident-free day for the thousands of riders – most with little or no experience of high-speed riding – who blast their way along the island's twisting mountain roads? From our vantage point at the Bungalow, high up on the mountain section of the course, we watch a stream of motorcyclists speeding by. Some riders are displaying L-plates, and others are carrying children as pillion passengers. In the TT festival's worst year, 1993, 10 lives were lost. Compare this with the progress made in reducing overall motor sport casualties in recent years.

Edmund King, executive director of the RAC Foundation, says: 'When you get to the stage where there's a risk of dying in order to have a bit of fun, then the wisdom of doing it must be questioned.

Simon Potter watches amateur motorcyclists risk all on the Isle of Man's Mad Sunday.

There are safer ways to have fun on two wheels, or indeed on four wheels.'

Police say they have made the course safer. A seemingly obvious step has been taken – the course has been made one-way instead of having cars, or even trucks, driving along it in the opposite direction. This followed a number of head-on collisions, brought about mostly by foreign riders forgetting which side of the road they should be on.

There have been other safety improvements. There are fat air cushions and straw bales on as many hazards as possible, an array of temporary speed limits and a high-profile police presence to ensure compliance with speed limits where they exist. Many of the island's 500 miles of roads have no limit.

Not surprisingly, Mad Sunday participants are delighted the event exists. Pete McConnell from Scotland says: 'Imagine going to watch a Formula One race, then streaming onto the track next day for a blat.'

Traffic policeman Keith Kinrade is on duty throughout the day, ready to respond to any emergency. 'Mad Sunday is unique,' he says. 'Today it's going well, the majority of people are behaving themselves. That's all we want.'

Across at Noble's hospital, for which 'high-velocity trauma' injuries are a key area of expertise, casualty teams stand by ready to deal with any riders who are brought in. By lunchtime there have been mercifully few incidents, but suddenly the police radio crackles into life.

A colleague announces a crash at Creg Ny Baa, a point on the course notorious for unseating even the most skilled riders. Today's smash sounds serious; the rider is unconscious, the police say he needs oxygen. An ambulance is on its way.

David Cretney, the Isle of Man tourism minister, is in favour of keeping Mad Sunday. 'I am continually lobbied by those who support an all-island speed limit, but my feeling is that we should focus on anyone who drives or rides dangerously,' he says.

Banning Mad Sunday would effectively require a closure of every island road, say the local authorities. They don't seem to consider enforcing a sensible speed limit.

Eugen Soboda, a German traffic policeman, is helping to deal with any incidents involving German riders. He watches with a pained expression. 'Skill levels here today have been crazy, bad and low,' he says. 'This could never happen in Germany. They would stop it within one minute.'

Delia Cope was asked by a friend to provide volunteer medical support at the TT event.
She describes her experiences in an internet article.

A MEDIC'S TT 1994 by Dr Delia Cope

So, Shane says to me "You're interested in motorbikes and medicine – fancy going to the TT races as part of the medical team?" Fine I say, next thing I know I'm doing 70 mph on the M6 breezing past Birmingham traffic on my rust bucket Honda 450 Nighthawk (don't buy one!) chasing a growing pack of bikes loaded up with tents, kitbags and people. Shane has opted out at this stage. Liverpool arrives and 300+ bikes embark onto the Isle of Man Steam Packet ferry (£111 return, 1 person + bike – a bit pricey). The Liver building fades into the Sunday night haze – beautiful. I get talking to lots of lads on the boat and the realisation dawns: bikes, men, leather – the perfect holiday!

Arrive at the Isle of Man, Douglas and eventually find the house I'm staying at. For the 2 week duration of the TT races people take in paying guests on a B&B basis which is a good way of getting to know the 'real island people'.

Monday morning, and picking up my medical gear I decide to take a tour of the famous road racing TT course. Call me naïve, but I never knew it was so varied, steep hills, mountain conditions, village roads, hairpins. I pootled clockwise around from Douglas, averaging 40 mph – feeling pretty cool – until I got overtaken on the inside by a Kawasaki 750 doing 100+ mph. (There is no speed limit outside the villages, which is one of the great attractions of the place.) Over Snaefell mountain I froze and was glad to get back to the seaside of Douglas for a cup of tea and a chat.

The work was good. I was posted at various positions around the 37 mile course for the duration of the practices (5–7.30am) and races (3–6pm or 6–9pm). I got to talk to lots of locals acting as marshalls – regaling me with stories of past TTs. Only once in my 7 days did I have to deal with a severely head injured rider – at Sarah's Cottage, a notorious hill bend with an unusual camber. The lad was stable on ITU when I left the island.

I had a fantastic week. Highlights include 3 hours up on the mountain with an 85 year old Matchless rider who explained Life, the Universe & Everything biker style, a cruise on a Virago 1100 (yes, I do want one), a zip through town on a Ducati Monster (nice frame, shame about the price), a drunken conversation with a lovely policeman at 4am about the pros and cons of BMWs for police use, and dancing the night away with the Macclesfield lads.

It was my first TT and it won't be my last. I didn't meet many independent women bikers – the few women that were there were on pillion. I really would recommend it thoroughly. I got to use my 450 in conditions quite different from home. I now feel more confident to move up to a bigger bike. The races are brilliant fun and the atmosphere electric at times. It also in some way restored my faith in men bikers – I was there a week as a single woman biker and was treated courteously, never patronised and given every consideration possible.

Reading and response

Answer the following questions.

Look at the newspaper report.

A1. According to the newspaper report, list ten reasons why motorcyclists take part in
Mad Sunday on the Isle of Man.   [10]

A2. How does Simon Potter try to persuade us that Mad Sunday should be banned?   [10]
In your answer, comment on:
- headline and picture
- what is said
- how it is said.

Now look at the internet article.

A3. What impressions to you get of Dr Cope from this article?   [10]
Consider:
- what she did
- what she saw
- who she met.

**To answer the next question you will need to consider both the report by Simon
Potter and the internet article by Dr Delia Cope.**

A4. Simon Potter and Dr Delia Cope both write about TT motorbike racing
on the Isle of Man. Compare what they have written.   [10]
You should look at:
- who the texts are aimed at
- the content – what the texts are about
- the choice of language
- the effect on the reader of each text
- the overall quality of presentation.

——————————————— **Tips before you start** ———————————————

*The Reading section of Paper 2 presents different problems from Paper 1. There are two
texts to read, so you have to be very purposeful. Skim the texts for general understanding,
then go to the questions and let them focus your reading. In other words, re-read the texts
when you have understood what the question requires. Make sure you are clear which text
is which – in this case, one is called a report and the other is called an article. Try not to
get them mixed up, especially when you are directed to one or the other for a new question.*

Take about 50 minutes for this section, giving roughly equal time to each question.

A1. The first word here is 'List...' so do as it says! Hunt down ten points from the newspaper
report that look like reasons for motorcyclists choosing to take part in Mad Sunday. Write
them down as bullet points as efficiently as possible. This is a 'search and find' question
and you need to get off to a good start here with a high score, because there will be more
difficult questions later. It is worth pointing out, however, that the 'search and find'
question on the Foundation tier will not necessarily be the first question on the paper –
always be alert to the wording of the question.

A2. This is an important question. You should certainly expect a question on persuasive
techniques in this non-fiction and media reading section. In any texts used in this section,
there will be an element of 'selling', often a product that you can buy from the shops, but
just as often an idea or a point of view that you might be persuaded to support. In Simon

Potter's report, he is hoping surely to make an impact on you when writing about the bikers and their activities on the roads. You do not have to agree with him, but you need to explore what he is saying, as well as how he is saying it. What tricks is he using? What response is he hoping to provoke? Understanding persuasion is a high-level skill, so think about your response – don't dive in too quickly. Use the bullet points below the question to help you.

A3. At this point in the sequence, you switch to the internet article. It is clear that the question is about Dr Cope, the writer of the article, but the key to a good answer is to respond to the word 'impressions'. You must try to draw out some views and opinions on the writer, based fairly on the evidence of her account of her trip to the TT races. It is not a question of liking her or not liking her, more a case of 'what kind of person she is'. The bullet points below the question again should help you.

A4. There will always be a 'comparative' question in this section, because that is the reason for having two texts rather than one – **but** it will not be the 'same' question every year. In this case, the instruction is 'Compare the ways...' . It is **not**, for example, 'Which of these two do you prefer?' Cross-referencing between two texts is another important skill and it is closely linked with organisation. You need to be clearly organised, so decide how you will approach it – because time is short, the best way is undoubtedly to consider the bullet points one-by-one, making a comparison between the texts each time. The quality of the comparisons is, of course, the most important thing.

Exploring responses

A1. Ten reasons why motorcyclists take part in Mad Sunday:
1. They can race on public roads.
2. There is no speed limit for their races.
3. There is no need for a special licence.
4. There is no need for special training.
5. They are not 'hassled' by the police.
6. They can see what it is like to drive at speeds of up to 150 mph.
7. They can test the TT circuit.
8. They have the opportunity to test their machines.
9. They have the opportunity to test their reflexes.
10. Anybody is able to enter – even learner drivers.

This is not the easiest of search and find questions, because you have to look far and wide in the report for the reasons. You may have to 'split some hairs' to get the full set, but the important thing here is to aim for ten distinct points. Be greedy for marks. Do not waste time explaining each reason – the question does not require it.

A2. The headline pulls no punches with a direct reference to death, and a sense of certainty about it. The picture reinforces speed and danger with a biker with one wheel off the ground. In his report, Potter tries to persuade us that Mad Sunday should be banned by saying that it is causing "numerous deaths" and "growing controversy". He addresses the readers directly (Imagine...) and persuades them to believe it is true there is a place where the riders have "no speed limit, and no need for special licences or training". The readers then share Potter's disbelief on discovering that this is not a fictitious event, but a part of the TT races on the Isle of Man.
    Potter seems shocked that "anybody, however poorly trained, can

get on the circuit and drive at speeds of up to 150 mph" and the reader feels just as shocked, even more so with the statistic that 200 people have been killed in these races since 1907.

Potter uses a rhetorical question in his article, forcing the reader to agree with him that it is dangerous to allow these races to continue when the course contains "unforgiving obstacles" that would virtually guarantee death for any rider who collided with them. Potter says he has actually witnessed this and the reader shares Potter's amazement that some racers have "L-plates, and others are carrying children as pillion passengers". Potter then introduces the ironic fact that although motorsport is generally safer these days, in one year 10 lives were lost at the TT races. This makes the reader feel very angry because, according to Potter, Mad Sunday "has the full approval of the authorities". To illustrate this, Potter includes a quote from the Isle of Man tourism minister, who does not want a speed limit to be introduced, because he wants to keep the visiting bikers happy.

Potter creates the impression to the reader that the authorities are uncaring about safety. He includes the claim from the police that they have made the course safer, but says "seemingly obvious" to make the police's decision to make the course one-way as unworthy of praise or recognition from the public. Potter creates the impression that previously on Mad Sunday – before this rule was enforced – it was simply suicidal. This again makes the Isle of Man authorities appear incompetent.

Overall, Simon Potter tries to shock the reader by the way in which he presents the facts simply. The facts speak for themselves. He is critical of the attitudes of the organisers who seem casual about death. To strengthen his case, he includes comments from the RAC and a German (!) traffic policeman, who both think that Mad Sunday is far too dangerous.

You need to approach this task logically to see how the report works – the headline and picture give some impact to the story, but it is the text that offers the persuasive argument and the writer that offers the persuasive techniques. This student's reference to Potter's direct address, the rhetorical questions, the statistics, the tone of shock and disbelief, the quotations all serve to show that the report has been read, however quickly, from beginning to end. This answer very clearly addresses the issue of 'How...?' and contains sensible comments throughout, backed up by appropriate detail from the text.

A3. Dr Cope gives the impression that the TT races are brilliant for anyone with a passion for motorcycles. Her article is littered with references to makes and models of motorcycles, which shows that she is a real fan of these machines. She does not fit the stereotypical image of a female doctor and she is clearly excited by the idea of spending two weeks on the Isle of Man with only "bikes, men, leather". This to her is the "perfect holiday", which implies that motorcycles form a large part of her life. Obviously, this means that giving medical support at the TT races is ideal for her.

As Dr Cope herself says, "Call me naïve". This sums up her whole attitude to the TT races. She obviously has had little experience of visiting islands, because she explains that she did not realise the course was so varied as she "pootled clockwise around from Douglas, averaging 40 mph". This statement seems odd – since most speed limits in built-up areas are 30 mph, 40 mph can hardly be described as "pootling" — driving slowly. She is then in awe of a Kawasaki 750 rider who overtook her on the inside (which is illegal!) while "doing 100+ mph". Dr Cope is completely oblivious to the dangers of the course and is instead impressed by all of the riders and their life threatening races. She even comments, "There is no speed limit...which is one of the great attractions of the place". This again shows that, although Dr Cope is obviously a well-educated woman, she has no common sense!

Dr Cope explains that "Only once in my 7 days did I have to deal with a severely head injured rider". She maintains a carefree attitude to this accident — focusing more on the stretch of course where the rider was injured than the actual injuries he sustained and his current condition. Despite dealing with this near fatal injury, Dr Cope insists "I had a fantastic week". The highlights for her included "a drunken conversation with a lovely policeman at 4 am". This statement leaves the reader wondering who exactly was drunk — Dr Cope, the policeman or both?

Generally, Dr Cope seemed more interested in who had the best machine at the TT races and how well each motorcycle handles than with the injuries of the riders — she has a fairly fatalistic view of danger. She is very enthusiastic about things, she lives life to the full, and probably believes in 'live today, die tomorrow'!

There is plenty to say about Dr Delia Cope and opinions may be divided — she could be regarded as adventurous or irresponsible or both. Opinion is free — in other words, there is not a right or wrong answer, but why not modify your opinion a little on occasions to consider alternatives? Use 'perhaps' or 'possibly' to extend an answer when you are developing a thoughtful argument. You are more likely to get a high mark if you are prepared to explore beyond the straightforward.

A4. In his report, Potter tries to appeal to readers who have limited experience of the TT races or those who feel strongly about road safety issues. In a sense, this should apply to anyone who drives, because these people should be most concerned with traffic safety. In contrast, Dr Cope's article is aimed at motorcycle fanatics. Even though she is a doctor, and the article is entitled 'A Medic's TT', there is nothing in this article that would appeal to members of the medical profession.

The content of Potter's report is on the whole descriptive, reporting in detail the risks involved with Mad Sunday. He attempts to present a balanced view of the races, even though his ultimate aim is to persuade the reader that Mad Sunday should be banned. His article includes plenty of quotes from a range of people involved with the races, which adds depth and support to his argument. Although occasionally he does poke fun at the authority figures, this is a serious article tackling a serious topic. Dr Cope's article is really the opposite of this. Her article is superficial and light-hearted. She leaves out any real detail about the Isle of Man or the races or anyone involved. Her commentary focuses solely on herself and her reactions to the races. She is apparently oblivious to other people's experiences of the races, including one unlucky rider who suffered a severe head injury. The majority of her article is focused on the motorbikes around her. She seems completely uninterested in her role as a member of a medical team and any issues of safety are unimportant to her. This is in contrast to Potter's report, where rider safety is of paramount importance.

In general, Potter's report is more persuasive because it is well focused on the dangers of Mad Sunday. Throughout his report, Potter continually presents evidence to show that Mad Sunday should be banned. Dr Cope's article is much less focused and its aim is not so clear. Although the overall effect is that the TT races are exciting, the general impression is that you would only really enjoy and appreciate the races if you can tell the difference between a Kawasaki and a Honda. Anyone who is not a motorcycle fanatic would not enjoy the TT races at all. This then makes her article less interesting to the general public than Potter's report, which presents a wider road safety issue.

Positioning yourself correctly is vital in this kind of comparative question. The bullet points help you to consider the audience and purpose of each text – only in the correct context can subtle points be made. Try to avoid saying superficial things, like 'The article is less interesting because it doesn't have a picture in it'! Good responses will make interesting comparisons (in discussion, rather than as a list) and will consider the effect of each text on the reader.

HIGHER TIER

Texts: leaflet and an extract from an autobiography

Read this leaflet about smacking by a 'Parents Against Smacking' action group.

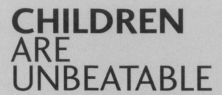

CHILDREN ARE UNBEATABLE

The dangers of smacking

Children should not be treated as smaller versions of adults. They are fragile and delicate and although they may seem resilient after countless bumps and scrapes in the garden, this does not mean that they cannot be seriously hurt by smacking. It is very difficult to judge how hard a smack is to a child. Something that may not feel that hard to an adult could be very painful indeed for a child.

There is also the danger of getting carried away. A parent may begin by lightly tapping their child on the back of the hand when they have done something wrong, but what happens when that no longer works as a deterrent for the child's bad behaviour? The parent may be tempted to use more and more aggressive forms of punishment to control the child. This is clearly not a good thing for either the parent or the child.

Why smacking doesn't work

Since children do most of their learning through imitating others, smacking has little or no effect on reducing aggressive behaviour. In fact, it is arguable that aggression would be increased because, even if there is no apparent physical damage, there may well be psychological damage caused from smacking your child.

Continual smacking may lead to resentment and poor relationships between parents and children. This is because smacking merely tells the child that he or she has done something wrong – it does not demonstrate the correct way of behaving and it does not explain the situation. If the child cannot understand what it has done wrong, then the bad behaviour is likely to be repeated.

Another problem with smacking is it very often leaves the parents feeling guilty for the way they have behaved towards their children. This often leads to parents over-compensating for this punishment by over-indulging their children in an attempt to reduce their own guilt. Obviously, this leaves the child feeling confused about whether or not they should carry out the bad behaviour again, if they know that in the long term they will gain rewards from it.

What are the alternatives?

Whatever you do as a parent, your child will occasionally be naughty. This is perfectly natural and is no reflection on your parenting skills. The key to successful learning is 'positive discipline'. This means getting the child to say sorry and then helping the child to put right whatever they did wrong. However, there are short-term solutions to minor instances of bad behaviour.

These include leading by example. Since children learn by copying, it is most important that you try to behave in appropriate ways around your child and set them a good example about how to behave. It is also helpful to explain to the child beforehand about the task you are going to do together. If the child knows what to expect and what to do, then fewer things can go wrong. It is always better to explain than to ignore. Ignoring bad behaviour usually leads children to try more and more naughty things. Another key thing is to be consistent in the way you reward and punish your child. Make sure similar behaviours are treated in the same way so that the child clearly understands what is expected of him or her.

Finally, try to avoid shouting at your child. Children usually shut out loud noises and do not pay attention to the message. A better method is to whisper because children's curiosity automatically becomes aroused and they want to know what is being said.

If all else fails, what then?

There are two more suggestions to be used as a last resort.

Isolation can be used, where the child is given a 'time out' either alone in their bedroom or in the corner of the room or sat in the middle of the floor. This can be very effective because children do not like to be excluded from the family in this way. However, if left for too long, the child can build up resentment towards the parent who placed them there.

Finally, if nothing else seems to be working, try holding your child while they have a tantrum. They will soon learn that the only way they will have freedom is by behaving quietly and doing as they are told.

Read this passage about parents and children from King of the Castle, *an autobiography by Martin Plimmer.*

See Barnaby *run!* See Barnaby *crash!* See Barnaby *bash his sister!*

There is no person so liberal as the child of the liberal. He does what he wants, when he wants, if not before. He pesters his parents relentlessly, like an underage insurance salesman. He gets inexplicably angry about the garlic bread.

Everybody *scream!*

His behaviour might be tolerable in the setting of the Siberian steppe, but we are in the echo chamber of Clapham Pizza Express, whose shiny marble surfaces amplify the toll of every baby, every volley of the Megazord war sled. Normally I don't like to eat while fighting is going on, but I have no choice.

It's not just Barnaby. It's India-Jane (*'Eeeeeeeeee!'*), and Portia too (*'Aaaaaaaaaaaaaaa!'*), and little Arkan (*'Skruuunk!'*). No problem: Pizza Express welcomes kids. All those wipeable areas of surface are just begging for it. Every Sunday, and particularly this Sunday, ten days before Christmas, the Pizza Expresses of London are magnets to the Espaces of Dulwich and Clapham and Putney, which arrive loaded with mobiles and bleepers and turbo buggies and fold-down cots – Whoops-ha-ha-sorry! – and Skogsblåbär baby bags and cussing plastic wrestlers and sound effects picture books and Power Ranger gloves that make a Taiwanese trumpet noise, and roller blades...

Roller blades?

Yes, Pizza Express welcomes roller blades.

These people are not poor. The adults are mostly ten years younger than me, dressed in quality casuals. Their pullovers are tied by the arms around their shoulders. The men have proper hairdos. Everything in their lives is under control, except their children. Welcome to the clattering classes.

What the children need, of course, is a good slap, but their super-dooper, all-smiling, super-absorbent liberal parents never slap their children. If you do hear a slap in Pizza Express, it's a Quattro Formaggi hitting the wall.

Here in liberal Clapham, the parental response is the forbearing smile, the whoops-ha-ha-sorry! mantra, and the dabbing ritual, with dabbing equipment retrieved from polka dot baby bags.

Curiously enough, these are exactly the sort of liberal middle-class people who came knocking on my door at 11.30 last night, complaining that my music was invading their right to silence (they're well up on their rights), and threatening to call the Lambeth Noisy Neighbour Police, who would come round and clamp me in muffs.

'But Ned Sublette is really rather good,' I told the man disingenuously, 'although at first it can seem an awkward coupling of Texan cowboy with Cuban percussion.'

'It's not the musical hybrid we object to,' he said, 'it's the fact we can hear it.'

'Oh really?' I said, pretending surprise. 'But it's Saturday night! Haven't you heard that Saturday night is for dancing?'

'Not when you have children trying to sleep.'

'Those are *your* children? I had Satan down as the father.'

***

Once, in a restaurant a long time ago, in a moment of infant fury, I lobbed a bread roll into my father's soup. There was a single exquisite, desperate moment of petrified satisfaction as my father's shirt deliquesced to oxtail, then everything was fear and pain. My father yanked me by the collar from my chair, dragged me through the kitchen, past lines of chefs who raised their cleavers in adult solidarity, and out into the back yard among the chicken heads and cabbage ends, where he slapped my legs extremely hard. I won't ever do it again, tempted though I am to tip my house red over Barnaby's head.

Reading and response

Answer the following questions.

Look at the leaflet.

A1. What reasons does the leaflet give for not smacking children?   [10]

A2. How does the leaflet try to persuade you that smacking is not a good way to discipline children?   [10]
Think about:
- the content of the leaflet
- the way the leaflet is presented
- the words and phrases used.

Now look at the extract from *King of the Castle*.

A3. What are Martin Plimmer's thoughts and feelings about children and parents?
How does he convey these thoughts and feelings?
Refer closely to the text in your answer.   [10]

To answer the next question you will need to consider both the leaflet and the extract.

A4. The leaflet claims that smacking a child is never justified. Using information from both the extract and the leaflet, explain how far you think this is true.   [10]

———————————————— **Tips before you start** ————————————————

The Higher tier questions in this section tend to have limited support in the form of bullet points. There is more emphasis expected on the writers' techniques than in the Foundation tier and less opportunity to spot and list points, although one question (often the first one, as here) allows students to accumulate credit steadily. The texts themselves will generally be a little more taxing in terms of language and/or subject matter.

A1. This question does allow you to list the reasons given for not smacking children, but you need to take some care that these are well defined and logically expressed. It is vital that the points are found in the text, not based on general knowledge.

A2. This question, especially in the light of question A1 concentrating on 'reasons', requires you to focus on 'how' the leaflet tries to persuade. This particular text is quite a demanding read, so it should push you into good habits of tackling language features with some determination, rather than settling for points about layout, pictures and headlines. These all count, of course, but they must not be allowed to dominate.

A3. The Martin Plimmer text is entertaining, but not straightforward. It is probably harder to appreciate than the leaflet, because irony is very difficult to pin down on occasions. You may have to steer around some of the more demanding details that are part of the cleverness of the writing in order to get the main thrust of the writer's attitude to children. You need to select and highlight what you see as the main evidence for his beliefs and avoid representing his views simplistically.

A4. This question requires cross-referencing of the two texts in a way that brings together the ideas of both. You need to organise information from the leaflet and slot in points of comparison and contrast from the extract. The way the question is formulated should help you to get an explanation going, but make sure you engage with each of the texts. As with the Foundation tier, you must be alert to the different types of 'comparison' question that you could be faced with in your final exam.

Exploring responses

A1. Ten reasons for not smacking children:

1. Children are fragile and delicate
2. They can be very seriously hurt by smacking
3. It is difficult to judge how hard a smack is to a child
4. There is a danger of getting carried away
5. Smacking has little or no effect on reducing aggressive behaviour
6. There may be psychological damage to the child, even if there is no physical damage
7. It may lead to resentment and poor relationships between parents and children
8. Smacking merely tells the child that it has done something wrong, it does not explain the situation
9. Parents feel guilty after smacking their children
10. There are many other successful alternatives to smacking, such as using short periods of isolation

The points above work perfectly well in a list, because each one in turn is clear and coherent. On the Higher tier, top marks would only be awarded if there was a thorough and relevant selection, with shape, coherence and a clear focus. In other words, at this level, there are no lucky hits!

A2. This is a very orderly, clear leaflet that begins with a clear headline (with a double meaning) in support of children and has a series of logical sub-headings. The presentation signals very clearly which side of the argument is being supported here, namely ANTI-smacking. Part of its persuasive power is the way it instructs parents directly.

Firstly, the leaflet explains the physical impact of smacking. It describes children as "fragile and delicate", implying they should be handled with care. The leaflet warns that "Children should not be treated as smaller versions of adults". It adds that "There is also the danger of getting carried away". It alarms parents that they may begin to use more and more violent methods of punishing their children if gently tapping them on the hand doesn't work. This obviously plays on the parents' worst fears.

The leaflet then explains the psychological effects of smacking. This sends a clear warning to parents that even if there seem to be no physical signs of damage, such as bruising, the child could still be injured emotionally. The leaflet goes on to explain in detail what is meant by "psychological damage"; "Continual smacking may lead to resentment and poor relationships between parents and children". This again plays on parents' fears of an unhealthy and unloving long-term relationship with their children.

As if this wasn't a powerful enough message, the leaflet goes on to explain the consequences for parents of "feeling guilty" for smacking and suggests they will end up buying their children expensive gifts by way of an apology. They use this exaggeration to make a further point that the child will become confused!

The leaflet offers for balance a lot of suitable and practical alternatives to smacking. There are enough alternatives in the leaflet to ensure that at most parents would use smacking only a last resort. This section reassures parents that "your child will occasionally be naughty", but the basis of these alternatives is what the leaflet gives as the catchphrase "positive discipline". The suggestions range from helping the child to put right whatever it did wrong (e.g. mopping up a spilled drink) to encouraging parents to always behave in a pro-social way in front of their children. This seems like a tall order for most parents, who are after all only human, but the leaflet seems to skip over this point. Each alternative to smacking is accompanied by an explanation of why this behaviour is a more appropriate form of punishment and how it is successful. The final words of encouragement ("If all else fails, what then?") are more extreme forms of punishment: isolation and "holding your child while they have a tantrum". Again, the rationale behind these suggestions is included, so that parents are persuaded into thinking that smacking is not a suitable punishment when there are so many other more appropriate options available.

In some respects this is a fairly conventional 'single issue' leaflet that tries to persuade you to take an unconditional point of view. It uses what are called 'stick and carrot' methods of persuasion. It warns and frightens you (beats you with a stick!), but also encourages you (offers you a carrot!). The answer above has a clear balance of detailed reading and exploration of ideas.

A3. Martin Plimmer gives the very clear impression that children today are out of control and that their parents are largely to blame for being too soft with them. It is difficult to say just how serious he is, but he writes almost maniacally in a Mr Angry style to recreate scenes of chaos that he has witnessed. He uses lots of imagery of children squabbling and messing with food and upsetting each other. He overdoses on onomatopoeia in the first few lines (Crash! Bash! Eeeeeeeee! Aaaaaaaaaaa! Skruuuunk!) and he must have had more fun writing than experiencing it. He creates a noisy, untidy scene through the haphazard, unpredictable way the piece is written, with extremes of sentence length and sprinklings of exclamation marks.

Children, according to Plimmer, always get their own way, ("He does what he wants, when he wants, if not before".) To make things worse, Plimmer implies that all of this bad behaviour is without a real cause, "He gets inexplicably angry about the garlic bread". From this it appears that children are uncontrollable, aggressive irrational beings. He criticises parents by strong implication, because they are too liberal. Far from the kids being liberal and rational, they are primitive and animal in their behaviour. Plimmer blames the parents, by suggesting they are indulgent, neglectful and only interested in themselves. Little details of fashion (pullovers and hairdos) give away their inept, conceited lifestyle, but Plimmer crushes them as parents with "Everything in their lives is under control, except their children." The tables are turned when the neighbour can't get his children to sleep because of Plimmer's loud music.

Plimmer believes that children should have a "good slap" rather than a "forbearing smile", but he is undoubtedly exaggerating his position greatly to make a satirical point about the new generation of parents. He presents this as hilarious slapstick, and sets himself up as a Victor Meldrew figure, but you can tell that he is seriously irritated by all this sloppy parenting, especially because these are educated people and they should know better.

When responses 'take off' like this one, the understanding seems total from the start, but there is sometimes less detail than there is from a more systematic, pedestrian answer. This response cuts through the detail to the overview and launches into high-level perceptions about the content and style of the passage. Though the answer operates successfully on different levels, the appreciation of slapstick and satire far outreaches the spotting of onomatopoeia!

A4. The leaflet is idealistic. It claims that you should never smack your child, which is probably a fair ideal to hold, but it is not convincing when it deals with the way children behave and the way parents should discipline them. Martin Plimmer brilliantly exposes the lack of realism in the leaflet, by describing the way children do behave, and clearly he believes their behaviour is caused by the lack of threat of a smack or as he calls it a 'slap'. However, he also believes that the young generation of parents are hopeless because they often do not have any inclination to discipline their children at all. Instead, they turn a blind eye to bad behaviour in public and allow their kids to irritate others by things like throwing food around restaurants. Parents-against-smacking would say that their whole belief is based on a package, that they are not against discipline, just against smacking and that parents should not be allowing their kids to get into this unruly frame of mind.

Plimmer perhaps cannot make up his mind whether the fault lies with the kids or the parents, but he does end his text with a story of how his father 'slapped my legs extremely hard' after a similar incident in a restaurant. He doesn't believe that it did him any harm. The leaflet has no human touches in it. It is devoid of humour and real sympathy for parents. I doubt whether Martin Plimmer is much of a child beater. However, anti-smacking campaigners would argue that because he remembers this smacking incident in such detail so many years means that he has been psychologically damaged for life! Plimmer wouldn't agree and neither would most people. Plimmer seems to have common sense and moderation on his side.

There are points of obvious contrast to make about each text, but you also should take on the question in good faith and try to work out any common ground between the two. Neither text is in favour of bad behaviour, both are in favour of discipline; both are in favour of avoiding smacking. You have to work hard to reach a well-considered view of the issue, engaging subtly with the two texts. The answer to a question like this one need not be of great length – it is more important to think your way in to a winning position, than to write a very long answer.

BE AWARE!

In Paper 2 Section A of both tiers, the skills of NON-FICTION AND MEDIA READING include:

■ Listing points selected from the texts
■ Explaining viewpoints and attitudes found in texts
■ Analysing persuasive techniques
■ Cross-referencing information and ideas

DO

comment on selected and highlighted words and sentences

DO NOT

make vague, generalised comments about pictures and layout

PAPER 2 SECTION B – TRANSACTIONAL AND DISCURSIVE WRITING
Writing to *argue*, *persuade*, *advise* and writing to *analyse*, *review*, *comment*.
FOUNDATION TIER

Transactional writing is writing with a clear sense of purpose, audience and format, for example a letter, a report, a leaflet.

Discursive writing focuses on argument, opinion and discussion, but often requires the features of transactional writing too, for example a newspaper article.

The two forms overlap to such a great extent that both tasks in Section B of Paper 2 could easily fit into both categories.

Tasks: writing a letter and a magazine article

Answer question B1 and question B2.

In this section you will be assessed for your writing skills, including the presentation of your work. Take special care with handwriting, spelling, punctuation and layout.

Think about the purpose and audience for your writing.

A guide to the amount you should write is given with each question.

(Note: Question B1 in Paper 2 is often linked in theme or topic to the material in Section A of Paper 2. Refer back to the newspaper report and the internet article on pages 25–26 of this Revision Guide as you consider the following task.)

B1. Imagine you either live on the Isle of Man or are visiting the island.

You decide to write a letter to one of the Isle of Man newspapers arguing for or against banning Mad Sunday, the day when amateur motorcyclists are allowed to ride around the TT road racing course without a speed limit.

Write the letter.   [20]

The quality of your writing is more important than its length. You should write one or two pages in your [A4] answer book.

———————————————— **Tips before you start** ————————————————

A formal letter is required here, so you would be expected to supply a sender's address on the right and the address of the organisation receiving the letter on the left. Include the date and do not forget to sign off at the bottom. Regarding commas, be consistent. As for Yours sincerely/Yours faithfully, the latter is definitely more formal, but the rules have relaxed in recent times. Much more important is the body of the letter – the content of your argument. In this case, re-familiarise yourself with the arguments for and against Mad Sunday on the Isle of Man and make your case as persuasively as possible. You can refer to the report and/or article if you wish.

————————————

semi-formal letter writing. The student uses the newspaper and internet material but not in a way that casts doubt on the originality of the expression.

B2. Mobile phones and the internet (including e-mails and chatrooms) have produced major changes in society in the last ten years.

A magazine on sale to the general public wishes to print interesting and lively articles on the ways young people use these 'new' inventions.

Write an article reviewing the use of mobile phones OR the internet. [20]

The quality of your writing is more important than its length. You should write one or two pages in your [A4] answer book.

─────────────────── **Tips before you start** ───────────────────

Expect the second task in this section to be 'free-standing'. In other words, the topic will be independent of the rest of the paper and will be introduced in the question itself. This means that it certainly will be a general topic on which every student could reasonably be expected to have an opinion. You won't have to be an expert, but try to write your opinions down in a lively way, backing them up with evidence and sound reasoning. You may have a strong opinion or your views may be mixed and undecided – that doesn't matter. It is the quality and interest of your writing that counts. Supply a headline to strengthen the impression of an article, but do not worry about columns.

─────────

Exploring responses

B2. *The Future is Mobile*

It is hard to believe that less than ten years ago mobile phones were a rare thing. For starters, they were the size and weight of a large house brick with an aerial that could probably pick up television signals. Fortunately, in the twenty-first century, mobile phones are tiny, so small that they can be lost down the back of a settee.

For teenagers, mobile phones are a fashion accessory — funky covers, mobile phone holders, etc. This, however, has given children something to bully others about. Have you got the latest model? Look, he's got the 3310 — that's so out of date! If you don't have the latest phone, then forget it!

This naturally is a cause of concern for parents, when they are presented with demands for phone cards from their spotty teenager. It raises the issue not only of at what age should children be given mobile phones, but also who should pay the bills? Should children under the age of ten have mobile phones? The gut instinct is to say no; that they are too young and irresponsible to look after such an expensive "toy". But the mobile phone offers the fantastic advantage of enabling parents to get in touch with their children whenever they want to, wherever their children might be. Surely this peace of mind is worth the expense. If a bus fails to turn up, the young person can ring home immediately and avoid distress on both sides.

You can be reached anywhere, any time. Although this is clearly not always a good thing, young people do not appear to mind, though even the most thick-skinned individual squirms a little when their phone goes off in a lesson or at the cinema. It can be irritating for others, but it is hardly a reason for opposing the whole existence of the technology.

Exploring responses

B1.

The Old House
72, High Street
Ramsey

23rd May, 2003

The Editor
Isle of Man Herald
40, Main Road
Douglas

Dear Editor,

I would like to draw your attention to the annual TT races, and more especially the day of racing known as "Mad Sunday". There has recently been an outcry against this event in the press and among non-motorcycle enthusiasts. I would like to express my support for Mad Sunday; I believe it is an essential part of the TT races. Without Mad Sunday, I do not believe that the TT races would attract as many visitors, tourists and spectators to our island.

Mad Sunday needs to be preserved; it is the only opportunity for many motorcyclists to complete the TT course. If Mad Sunday was banned, then these amateur motorcyclists would race around the Isle of Man at all times of the year. Surely this is far more dangerous for both the motorcyclists and the pedestrians and other road users. Although I realise that Mad Sunday does produce some casualties, paramedics and other emergency services are on immediate stand-by to offer their assistance in these accidents. This additional assistance is not as readily available when the TT races are over, meaning anyone attempting the course outside of Mad Sunday is in significantly more danger.

Complaints have been made that the TT races are unnecessarily dangerous, but in recent years new safety precautions have been introduced. The course is now one-way only and all non-race traffic has been stopped from using the course while the races are being held. These safety provisions have significantly decreased the risks to riders and other road users.

Mad Sunday is a unique motorcycling experience. Inexperienced motorcyclists and even motorcyclists without licences are allowed to complete the course. This gives amateur riders a real taste of how exciting motorcycling can be and offers people who have never ridden a motorbike before the opportunity to try — on possibly the greatest motorcycle course in the world. How could anyone fail to fall in love with motorcycling after that? Mad Sunday should not be banned.

Yours faithfully,

A. Ryder

This letter is of a good length and it has a coherent, logical and fairly persuasive argument for keeping Mad Sunday. You could, of course, easily construct the argument against it! The paragraphs are convincingly developed and the whole piece shows a pleasing command of the skills of argumentative writing and

PAPER 2 SECTION B – TRANSACTIONAL AND DISCURSIVE WRITING
Writing to *argue, persuade, advise* and writing to *analyse, review, comment.*
FOUNDATION TIER

Transactional writing is writing with a clear sense of purpose, audience and format, for example a letter, a report, a leaflet.

Discursive writing focuses on argument, opinion and discussion, but often requires the features of transactional writing too, for example a newspaper article.

The two forms overlap to such a great extent that both tasks in Section B of Paper 2 could easily fit into both categories.

Tasks: writing a letter and a magazine article

Answer question B1 and question B2.

In this section you will be assessed for your writing skills, including the presentation of your work. Take special care with handwriting, spelling, punctuation and layout.

Think about the purpose and audience for your writing.

A guide to the amount you should write is given with each question.

(Note: Question B1 in Paper 2 is often linked in theme or topic to the material in Section A of Paper 2. Refer back to the newspaper report and the internet article on pages 25–26 of this Revision Guide as you consider the following task.)

B1. Imagine you either live on the Isle of Man or are visiting the island.

You decide to write a letter to one of the Isle of Man newspapers arguing for or against banning Mad Sunday, the day when amateur motorcyclists are allowed to ride around the TT road racing course without a speed limit.

Write the letter. [20]

The quality of your writing is more important than its length. You should write one or two pages in your [A4] answer book.

────────────────────── **Tips before you start** ──────────────────────

A formal letter is required here, so you would be expected to supply a sender's address on the right and the address of the organisation receiving the letter on the left. Include the date and do not forget to sign off at the bottom. Regarding commas, be consistent. As for Yours sincerely/Yours faithfully, the latter is definitely more formal, but the rules have relaxed in recent times. Much more important is the body of the letter – the content of your argument. In this case, re-familiarise yourself with the arguments for and against Mad Sunday on the Isle of Man and make your case as persuasively as possible. You can refer to the report and/or article if you wish.

──────────

BE AWARE!

In Paper 2 Section A of both tiers, the skills of NON-FICTION AND MEDIA READING include:
- Listing points selected from the texts
- Explaining viewpoints and attitudes found in texts
- Analysing persuasive techniques
- Cross-referencing information and ideas

DO

comment on selected and highlighted words and sentences

DO NOT

make vague, generalised comments about pictures and layout

Mobile phones offer the fantastic opportunity for sending text messages, which is a service that the land-line cannot yet offer. A short text message, "C u l8r", can save a long tedious phone conversation and the message is received and understood instantly. With the latest advances in technology, it is now possible also to access the internet on WAP mobile phones. This means you can check your emails or surf the web on the bus to school.

This enables people to easily take their work home with them or stay in touch with people who may be hundreds or thousands of miles away. It also begs the question of what will be the next advance in mobile phones — television? DVD? Who knows? Whatever it is, you can bet all of the teenagers in the school-yard will be queuing up with their parents' hard-earned money to get one.

It is quite difficult to sweep across the short history of mobile phones. The material here is very largely relevant to the needs of young people and a positive outlook is maintained. The argument in favour of mobile phones is quietly built up through clearly expressed evidence. Some counter-arguments are easily brushed off by common-sense and good reasoning.

HIGHER TIER

*There are not always sharp differences in difficulty between Higher and Foundation tier
tasks in this section, but generally this is an area where the Higher tier can be a little
more demanding in terms of content and the extent of discussion. However, you could be
asked on either tier to write a letter, a factsheet, a leaflet, a report, a 'speech' or an
article.*

Tasks: writing a contribution to a radio phone-in and a magazine article

Answer question B1 and question B2.

*In this section you will be assessed for your writing skills, including the presentation of
your work. Take special care with handwriting, spelling, punctuation and layout.*

Think about the purpose and audience for your writing.

A guide to the amount you should write is given with each question.

*(Note: Question B1 in Paper 2 is often linked in theme or topic to the material in
Section A of Paper 2. You may find it helpful to refer back to the material on pages 32–4
of this Revision Guide.)*

B1. A radio station is having a phone-in debate about anti-social behaviour, particularly that
displayed by young people.

You decide you want to contribute. You know that you will have limited time on the air
and you need to organise your thoughts, so you prepare yourself by writing down what
you want to say.

Write your contribution to this radio programme. [20]

*The quality of your writing is more important than its length. You should write one to two
pages in your [A4] answer book.*

──────────── **Tips before you start** ────────────

*This task requires a speech in one of the less formal contexts, a radio phone-in. However,
standard English is still broadly expected, and punctuation and spelling are just as
important too. Do not regard this as a live transcript of a dialogue between presenter and
caller, but as a single, organised contribution with a coherent argument that either criticises
social behaviour or defends the public, especially young people. There may be opportunities
to include occasional features of spoken English, but do not resort to 'er' and 'um'!*

────────────

Exploring responses

B1. *I'm a first-time caller to a phone-in. I'm ringing this morning because
I'm angry about some of the nonsense talked so far. I think the
problem of selfishness in society lies with parents. There is no difference
between the way most young people behave and how their parents
behave in similar situations. If you grow up seeing your mum or dad
throw litter out the car in the middle of town or country, you're going
to do exactly the same when you get your first wheels. It's obvious. If
you grow up with a dog in the family that is allowed to foul the
pavement outside someone else's front door, then later in life you're
going to let your dog do the same.*

The reason that kids display incredible depth of awareness and concern about global issues is entirely because of schools and teachers, not parents. They know all about conserving and recycling and collecting money for Children in Need, but for most youngsters it is all about going blindly along with the crowd, rather than acquiring any values for life, because as soon as they arrive home from school they pick up mixed messages from their parents. 'You're bored? Well, stop moaning about it and stop getting under my feet. Go and play with your mates...' and off they go — for as long as they want, until they get tired, or hungry, or they want to watch their favourite TV programme. They can terrorise the community for a while, just as long as they are out of sight of their parents.

Perhaps it's a good thing in some ways, but there really isn't a divide these days between childish and adult behaviour. It's the adults, not the children, who dress up in fancy dress at test matches and, increasingly, the hooligan element in football is the well-to-do, bored, wannabee executive — in other words, someone with money. We even use the phrase 'adult toys', for goodness sake. So, when a car pulls up alongside you at the traffic lights and you suddenly find yourself enveloped in the sound of rap, look across and you may discover the guy next to you is not 17, but twice that age!

I heard sometime ago that the government were going to operate a 'zero tolerance' policy on anti-social behaviour, anything from fly-tipping to dropping your chewing gum on the street. On-the-spot fines for small offences and community service for persistent trouble-makers. There's kids of all ages that need to be grounded and have their pocket money stopped...

The above writing shows how standard English can meet colloquial English halfway to provide an effective style or 'voice' for a persuasive argument. It is actually quite a powerful weapon to be able to mix informal words with a more formal vocabulary, provided it is done deliberately and skilfully. This piece actually picks up the satirical, argumentative style of Martin Plimmer in 'King of the Castle' and uses examples of everyday behaviour to back up opinions.

B2. A magazine has invited readers of all ages to submit lively, entertaining articles about the recent craze for 'reality' television programmes.

Write an article reviewing 'reality' television. [20]

The quality of your writing is more important than its length. You should write one to two pages in your [A4] answer book.

——————————— **Tips before you start** ———————————

This task requires some awareness of purpose and audience. The brief introduction to the task places it in its wider context – 'the generation gap'. There is a challenge for students to respond with writing that is highly topical (the current obsession) to an audience that will presumably include people who are greatly puzzled by the attraction of reality TV.

——————————

Exploring responses

B2. *Escape to Reality*

I suppose it all started in the summer of 2000. For ten long weeks, Britain was united in its outrage that Nasty Nick dared to cheat on the live reality television show 'Big Brother'. Nick Bateman became a national hate figure and Craig Phillips, who challenged him over his behaviour, became our hero. Being a working class Liverpudlian carpenter, he represented the ordinary man, whereas Bateman, with his Oxbridge degree and posh accent, represented the oppressive middle classes. True television drama at its best. The nation was gripped. From the secret notes Bateman passed to fellow housemates to the kangaroo court style trial and ending with Bateman's tearful apology, it couldn't have been better if it was scripted. For good or bad, this series paved the way for a deluge of other reality television shows; each one more outrageous and more painful to watch.

In the year of the first 'Big Brother', Britain also sat and watched as fifty or so people were stranded on Taransay, a tiny remote and desolate island off the coast of Scotland. The most interesting event of island life was when a couple of sheep escaped from their pen and everyone had to run over the island trying to catch them. Thrilling! There seems to be a connection between reality television shows and abandoning people in remote places. 'Survivor' sees two teams of people battling it out on a tropical island somewhere in the Pacific for a prize of £1 million. There is always the sneaking suspicion that the contestants spend every night in a plush hotel that is located just off camera. This is particularly true for 'I'm a Celebrity Get Me Out of Here'. It is hard to believe that celebrities (or former celebrities, in this case) would agree to spend two weeks together alone in the heart of the Australian jungle without any comforts, like a make-up artist or personal assistant. It's hard to believe that these celebrities are not sipping cocktails and trying out the sauna once the cameras stop rolling. But this show still manages to attract huge viewing figures; this may be partly due to Ant and Dec's irreverent behaviour, which mostly involves mimicking the celebrities' idiosyncrasies, to the audience's constant wondering about what 'Fash' would be phobic about next!

This year, however, reality television shows seem to have lost their appeal. 'Big Brother 4', nicknamed 'Big Boring', had very little to offer its audience, with the contestants too scared that they would be booed by the audience on their eviction to say anything remotely controversial (or interesting). Likewise, BBC's 'Fame Academy', referred to as 'Lame Academy' by those unfortunate enough to have sat through an episode, has had decreasing ratings each week. So does this mean that we will see the end of reality TV shows? That is very doubtful. In an act of desperation, TV producers will come up with even more controversial and outrageous ideas.

But how much worse can these ideas get? We have already been given the opportunity to witness Jordan giving birth on the internet; America offers us 'Who Wants to Marry a Millionaire?' which, sadly, is exactly as it sounds. Channel 4 offered us the chance to watch the first live televised autopsy and ITV are currently running 'Don't Drop the Coffin', a reality TV show about funeral directors. It seems the whole spectrum of human life has already been covered in one way or another. I'm sure even my "delinquent and immoral" generation is concerned about what subject the reality TV show producers will choose next. All that remains to be said is, "Be afraid, be very afraid".

The knowledge of the subject in the above article is very impressive, but probably not exceptional, given the number of avid viewers of all ages. Whether or not the programmes are tedious, the actual review writing here is bright and thought-provoking. It informs, questions, argues, and entertains, all in quite sophisticated, controlled expression.

A NOTE ON THE LAYOUT AND FORMAT OF REPORTS AND LEAFLETS

The tasks included in this section are typical of those set in Paper 2 Section B of the WJEC English examinations. In addition, it is possible that you will be asked to write a formal report or a leaflet, so here briefly are the layout features of these two types of writing. Like the other categories, they also require clear, accurate expression as the main priority.

Reports
Formal reports, such as a report to the school governors on a proposal by the sixth form to organise a charity event, should be presented with a heading, a clear indication of who is writing the report and who is receiving it, and the date.

Bullet points and sub-headings will generally feature in reports but, above all, write carefully constructed sentences in standard English.

Leaflets (and factsheets)
When asked to write a leaflet in the examination, include a heading and sub-headings. Represent a picture with an empty box and a word or two inside the box.

Use bullet points (but do not overdo them). You can write in columns, but it is not necessary.

BE AWARE!

In Paper 2 Section B of both tiers, the skills of TRANSACTIONAL and DISCURSIVE WRITING include:
- Understanding different formats and layouts
- Awareness of audience
- Developing opinions and ideas effectively

DO
look carefully at the exact requirements of each task

DO NOT
neglect your quality of expression, including spelling

Tiers, grades and marks

Tiers – grades awarded

Foundation tier	G	F	E	D	C			
Higher tier				D	C	B	A	A*

There is a 'safety net' of 'an allowed E' for candidates who narrowly miss a grade D on the higher tier.

> You will not be entered for the Higher tier unless you are a clear C-grade candidate with a chance of a B grade.
> For the Higher tier:
> ♠ In Section A (Reading) of Paper 1 and Paper 2, the texts may be harder, questions will tend to test higher level skills, and there may be less support in the form of bullet points.
> ♠ In Section B (Writing) of Paper 2, the tasks may be more difficult.

Grades and marks

All tasks in the English exam(s) are either marked out of 10 or out of 20. The relationship between grades and marks is different for the Higher tier than for the Foundation tier.

Grade band	Foundation (/10) (/20)	Higher (/10) (/20)	Qualities in reading and writing
G/F	2–4 5–9	0–1 0–4	generalized; straightforward
E/D	5–7 10–14	2–4 5–9	clear; developing; supported
C/B	8–10 15–20	5–7 10–14	detailed; structured; sustained
A/A*		8–10 15–20	confident; subtle; precise